The Way of the Living Ghost

THE
WAY
of the
Living Ghost

JOHN ANDERSON

Folk Necromancy in Transmission, VOLUME 5

Revelore

SEATTLE
MMXIX

The Way of the Living Ghost

© John Anderson 2019.

Fifth volume of the Folk Necromancy in Transmission series conceived and curated by Dr Alexander Cummins and Jesse Hathaway Diaz.

Book and cover design by Joseph Uccello.
Cover art: "Cataract" by Bryan Paul Patterson, 2019.

ISBN 978-1-947544-19-2

Printed globally on demand through IngramSpark

First printed by Revelore Press in 2019

Revelore Press
220 2nd Ave S #91
Seattle, WA 98104
United States

www.revelore.press

Contents

Book Two
Dào Guǐ (道鬼)
The Ghost's Progress

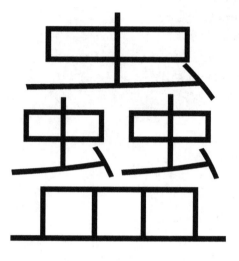

FOREWORD

There is a magical renaissance afoot, evoked in many projects seeking to unearth and restore context to the evolving, auto-poietic flowering of the mycelial net of ideas and practices. Dr John Anderson's Way of the Living Ghost is one of the fruiting bodies of the chthonic rebirth. And like the mushroom too, it may be in the most unexpected, and lowest of places, in the waste and the wastelands, that we chance upon the regenerative path that cycles back towards life.

It was no accident, it seems, that I met John in the first few days of his training in Chinese Medicine over a decade ago. In that time, I have been his teacher, supervisor, mentor, colleague, co-ceremonialist, and ultimately, friend. He pursued and completed a Master's, a doctorate, and has gone on to teach and write both within and without the Chinese medicine field. His doctoral capstone presages the work presented here: a groundbreaking assay of ghosts and spiritual parasites, and their traditional nosology, and treatment. He claims that our path towards friendship started with an off-hand reference to a twenty-sided die, or at least paladins. But in my memory, it may have been *Finite and Infinite Games*. Accidental? No, but certainly chance operations, synchronicities, and a throw of the dice.

As John notes in the Introduction, the present text shares the terse, laconic poetic style of the *Dao De Jing* (DDJ), but develops according to a different logic that offers a counterpoint to the balance and harmony esteemed in the original text. Both texts also develop and share a comfort with paradox. In this way, *The Way of the Living Ghost* enacts a pouring of old wine into new skins. It is as if the living ghost is embodied through its own disembodiment, and yet is less disembodied than its hungry ghost or non-corporeal counterpart. The living ghost paradoxically lives out the statement from DDJ 41: "The Way forward appears to move backwards." The Way out is through, and the Way through is down and in, not up and out: the disrupted and perverted hungers of the ghostly, the disenfranchised, disowned, shadowy, isolating individuation is only furthered by the outward turn in the act of consuming and taking in the barrage of stimuli from without. Like Anna Tsing's mushroom at the end of the world, the fruit erupts in the spaces most devastated by the totalizing post-industrial Anthropocene; fungus and root establish their symbiosis in the blasted landscape. The living ghost defiantly exhausts itself in a trickster logic of transmigration.

Becoming-Ghost, Becoming-Dead as the living ghost subverts the natural apotheosis of the special dead, and injects a poison into clock-time. Since this can take the form of more material insults from without, we speak of Gu (蠱) poisons, a kind of spiritually infused toxicity. When the insult arises from the social sphere, then we speak more properly of ghosts. When either of these gain purchase in the system, the yin of form separates from the yang of function, and vacuity invites chaos. Thus, it is the improperly venerated dead that compromise the individual expression of the body-social, and the improperly metabolized substance that compromises the visceral body in the Living Ghost. But Chinese medicine, with its potential for a rigorous non-dualism, recognizes that the treatment is not to allopathically oppose the process, but often to stimulate the process towards an enantiodromia. When Yang becomes chaotic, it is by stimulating and strengthening the yang function that order is restored to the yin form. This is essentially the act of restoring a disruption of the proper relation between space, time, rhythm and direction: it is a form of resuscitation of the Breath of Life.

The fundamental paradox at the root of the living ghost is trading that which is temporal for the spatial. It implies allowing that which is an expression of duration to be localized in the flesh, or the being to be subverted in its becoming, precisely through its own visceral drives. And therefore, one way of looking at Dr Anderson's prescription offered in this text is to paradoxically employ a sense of time to treat a disorder of time. The appropriate process is the embodiment of the Spirit (Heaven) through the Soul (Human) and Body (Earth) and in a fully embodied state. Conversely, the opposite process is rather from below, with the drives of the body striving to overtake Soul and Spirit—paradoxically the opposite of embodiment. Those earthly drives that even survive and coalesce as that which survives

Life are the manifestations of the ghost. Those which draw this otherworldly, energy into the earthly physical as a substance to be consumed manifest as the living ghost. Rather than the concretization of the spiritual, there is a crystallization of it: calcification and calculus, conjoined.

As painful as it may be, Anderson points out that we may all have qualities of the Living Ghost. He unabashedly directs us to assess the reality of our ghostliness if we ever hope to step off the path of the Living Ghost. The limiting of the temporal with the characteristics of the spatial, is like limiting the living with the characteristics of the dying. As soon as we break through those limits, time-freedom can be experienced as the flow within us that allows the dead to be themselves and yet ever-present in the bodily experience. Concentration is a plaything in the hands of a greater awareness, and while the former is finite, that latter is infinite. Through contemplation the two are temporarily joined and a deeper communion becomes possible. By stopping in time, we awaken to its duration, where past, present, and future are equally available. By truly looking within, we perceive the true face of the other, and restore the potential for living connection.

By perceiving the Other within, we perceive the Self. As we perceive the Self we see the Other without. The Living Ghost becomes the withering body that allows the deepest mycelial connections to burst forth, mediating between the seen and the unseen; recognizing the living, animated communication, and learning how to skillfully navigate its channels of manifestation is the greatest act of magic possible: the transmutation of death into life—the transformation of the Living Ghost into the living. Dr John Anderson invites us not just to participate in a magical renaissance, as much as a truly magical resurrection of ourselves.

Brandt Stickley, L.Ac
Assistant Professor
College of Classical Chinese Medicine
National University of Natural Medicine
PORTLAND, OREGON

EDITORS' PREFACE

The book you are now reading is a welcome and proud addition to the roster of Revelore Press' Folk Necromancy in Transmission series, and one that allows us as editors the slightest of opportunities to, well, editorialise on some of our wider goals and how we think this current work addresses, explores, and explicates our vision for this series. Please permit a moment to relive our own past; as indeed a ghost might.

The series began by publishing an anthology centering upon the history, mythos, and magic of one Saint Cyprian of Antioch, the infamous sorcerer-saint of nigromancy. It gave us ample opportunity to consider how a hagiography itself can be a living shade, shifting and adapting, and how the crossed beams of death and infamy can split a figure's shadow into many shades.

This was closely followed up with a collection of the Portuguese folk tales concerning this sorcerer-saint's equally infamous grimoire. To be clear, this was not another collection of texts declaring themselves to be the actual tome of Cyprian's black magic.

In many tales of its sinister power, the True Black Book of Cyprian can *only* be read in dream and copied out in part, after all. Instead then, we were delighted to invite José Leitão's cartography of the *Immaterial Book*; that is, the legends of Cyprian's grimoire embedded in the Iberian locales of enchanted treasures and the *mouras* who guard them. This work helped explicate how a folk necromancy of a text deals not only with the text itself, but the shadows it casts in popular imagination, cultural expressions, and mythic weight.

My own *Book of the Magi* was our third release, a work dedicated not simply to specific histories of medieval and early modern magian cultic veneration or surviving and flourishing Epiphany customs and cakes (although there is a cake recipe, fear not), but towards the Magi as a loci about which one might cohere engagements with dead magicians.

Most recently we published *Svartkonstböcker*, Dr Thomas Johnson's masterwork on the Swedish Black Art Book tradition. A posthumous publication foreworded by Thomas' widower, this marked a further kind of exploration of text and the dead for the FNIT series, as well as being a monumental work of folk necromancy itself.

And so, finally, we come to this book, which I believe continues our explorations of both small quotidian and thoroughly singular "high ritual" encounters between the living and the dead. Because this unique work not only seeks to find the dead, but to find the ways of the dead *in* those of the living.

Ultimately you are about to read a work focused on learning not simply *about* ghosts, but learning *from them*.

So, what can be said of the living ghost, and what it can teach us? Let us begin with the simplest model of the ghost as emotive trace in physical space, as a tape-loop crackle of reified echo. The apparition retracing its steps along dusty corridors and walking through the walls where once were doors. Earthbound, unaware, and cyclical, un-living out a circuit as repetition blurs the sharp contrasts of novelty into an undifferentiated loop. Such loops stack and bend to chain links, feeding on little more than inertia, and thus ever ravenous. The living ghost is what remains when the soul of someone is no longer there. An autopilot of consciousness. The automatic, the unexamined, the habitual, nay the habituating, the addictive; perhaps even the ideological.

Yet a ghost might be more than a recording, more than the mere groove of shade worn into our daily commute through Samsara. A ghost can be the telltale heart beating beneath floorboards; the Rorschachs of accusatory bloodstains. Each ghost may rattle chains back to what bound it in undeath, and may sing its threnody from its winding sheet music. A ghost is also what whispers back when straining to hear the deposition of the body, echoing out of its shell a eulogy of what was killed of it. A transparent remembrance, fading into that which is no longer quite felt, but still somehow missed. The absences that assert themselves as fluxing cold-spots barely a breath's breadth ever away.

What specters haunt the conscience of living in early twenty-first century Western civilisation? The answer seems to be: at the very least, ourselves. We are all the ghosts at the feast. Such a hauntology of our modern purgatories seems exactly what this Guidebook for the Habitually Unceasing seeks to explore. That it does so in the gallows humour of pitch-black sarcasm and cold irony is only appropriate. The word *demonstration* shares its root with *monster*: we may arguably learn more—shocked into epiphany—from a horror than a hero.

Speaking as a professional diviner who helps clients frame their choices, it seems that many of us can feel more empowered in rejecting deliberately negative (even—if appropriate—cartoonish) characterisations than immediately submitting to proscriptions and injunctions. In moving past a negative we can remind ourselves of the values, goals, and the purposes we forge. "I'm not saying [adopts dramatic voice] *you will never love again*, but do you think perhaps now is more a time to focus on X?" You may have already noticed just how many sentences of this very preface are framed as "not (merely) X, but Y." Sometimes it seems we do well to start from a recognition of what we are rejecting or expanding upon.

To know the ways of a living ghost is to be able to recognise and diagnose our own actions. When are we simply going through the motions? When are we, however unconsciously, smothering our hope? When are we bound by our fetters more than enlivened by what we choose to bond with? When and how do we make our worlds greyer? Healing must begin with diagnosis. A war must be fought on proper intel, especially an inner war. And thus, speaking as an editor of the Folk Necromancy in Transmission series, I can firmly say I am delighted to welcome this etiology of the living ghost, this pathology of dulled hearts hungering for what lies beyond caged loops and ever-unfinished business, this monstrous pedagogy of wraiths.

Dr. Alexander Cummins
BROOKLYN, NEW YORK
September, 2019

Introduction

Heavy, plodding steps…
heels first, dragging mud and feces…
this is the endgame of your journey…
But…your journey will not end…

What you hold in your hands is nothing simple. It is a template for life as many of us now live it. It is both a preemptive Guidebook for the Habitually Unceasing, and a work about cessation. A Roadmap to a Modern Hell, and a means to Reprieve. You have at your fingertips, Dear Reader, a means by which to understand the place where you currently are, which you will cleave to hence, and, in short, how you've gotten to where you are. For some of you, it will also provide a means to Euthanatos, although this may be outside of the comfort zone of many of you, Readers, as there is something very important with which you must come to terms before you can begin to undo it.

This is the upshot.

If you are reading this right now, chances are very good that you may be a ghost.

* * *

This is a loaded assertion which ought to be unpacked, and some patience may be required on the part of the reader before this state is fully comprehended. Even more is required if this assertion is to be accepted, and even more still if it is to be rectified. You see, reader, we already have in our minds what we think "is" or "is not." Many concepts can have very different meanings to different people, and the term "ghost" is no exception. When we hear the term "ghost," we have several pictures to which we have been exposed to culturally, either in terms of popular expression, or in within the confines of deeper cultural constructs which may be found within various populations of people. Either of these manifestations can color our interpretations as well as what we do with this information.

For the vast majority of readers in the United States, and arguably Western modern culture as a whole, the first exposure to the unseen world exemplified by ghosts comes through exposure of the first sort (i.e., pop culture as embodied by movies and television shows), while much of the world outside of the modern Western milieu takes its cue from the deeper cultural constructs (myths, legends, and/or customs) as transmitted within families or smaller populations.

Ghosts in popular Western culture

In terms of westernized pop culture, we have several ready-made narratives. A ghost may be friendly or lonely and merely looking for friends with which to spend its existence (e.g., *Casper*). A ghost may be angry, looking to avenge those who have wronged it in the past, or even led to its demise (*Ghost*). A ghost may be evil in its drives, looking only to consume the essence or psyche of an unwitting victim. Indeed, a ghost may even wish to possess an individual in order to take over his or her body for any number of "nefarious means" which meet the ultimate goals of the evil entity. Other times we see a ghost as being a bumbling comedic venture used to make light of the afterlife (*Beetlejuice* or *Ghostbusters*), or as having "unfinished business" to which the unfortunate ghost must attend before it can make its long-awaited journey to the next place, wherever that may be.

Any one of these manifestations, be it the ominous chain-laden specter of Jacob Marley as presented in Charles Dickens' *A Christmas Carol*, or the laughable ectoplasmic corpulence of "Slimer" found in the Ghostbusters movie franchise. Each provide a convenient representation of ghostly spirits as commonly encountered within the Western culture. This is, however, only one group of popular representations.

Ghosts as they are encountered in many non-Western versions of popular culture tend to be far more alien in their appearance and methods, even if their inherent drives are somewhat similar to those encountered in the West.

Societal manifestations of ghosthood

On a cultural level, there is more depth to be had when discussing the broader topic of ghosts beyond their being manifestations of pop-culture, and it is here where the value of the ideas presented in this text tends to reside. That is, a ghost can take on many forms and even roles within a larger cultural setting, and these too, can take on positive or negative forms and connotations.

In cultures all around the world, a ghost may be seen as a protector spirit, associated with some particular person or population whose role it is to keep at bay unwanted influences or events who would cause harm to those persons. This can be seen in the view of spirits espoused by some forms of Western esoteric practice as well as indigenous beliefs found in North America. Indeed, from a larger perspective a ghost can be seen as providing protection to an entire population, providing talismanic power to a much larger group. This can be seen in the belief systems of the Shang and Zhou Chinese dynasties, with echoes still found today in parts of China, Taiwan, Singapore, as well as Tibet and Nepal and many other parts of Asia. Here, an ancestral spirit who has grown from its "humble" beginnings as a human ghost and has assumed the mantle of the spirit protector of an entire country, or region, or lineage. The ghost in this case has "worked its way up" from being a mere human spirit to becoming a lineage holder or geographic spirit. The worship of the Bā Xiān (八仙) or "Eight Immortals" is one example of a limited apotheosis at work. While this can affect a wider population, it is hardly personal, and protective measures aside, this type of spirit is less common in the modern setting than many other forms of spirit-being.

The most common manifestation of a "ghost" still found in many Asian cultures around the world today is that of the è guǐ (餓鬼), or "hungry ghost." This type of ghost, with this potbelly and elongated neck forms a classic image, and one which in many ways parallels the imagery presented in this text.

The è guǐ does not necessarily exemplify the qualities of wrath and retribution, expressed as a burning need for vengeance directed at a person or a group, in the same way that other categories of ghosts might. Here, there is a longing for inclusion, and the cultural lesson is centered on the value of belonging, charity, and benevolence. In the case of the è guǐ there is often just the need to be recognized and nourished by the living. The living person is then taught to be an exemplar of these virtuous qualities by taking care of the wayward spirit.

In other contexts, the ghost plays a cautionary role to warn against the dangers involved in the transgression of cultural norms and propriety in general. There are ghost stories meant to provide an illustration of what may occur should a person break certain rules. These stories, primarily expressed in the form of folktale and allegory, provide a means to communicate cultural norms in such a way that provokes a visceral response within the listener.

Contemporary manifestations of these themes are still found in Asian cultures at large and these ghostly currents are still deeply engrained. This is most easily observed in the customs surrounding the "care" and veneration given to deceased relatives. These deeper cultural expressions of ghosts both represent very different processes, although both are normative in their own ways.

Ghosts of the Ancestors

In the Shang dynasty, ancestral spirits were fed so as to keep the living within the good graces of the deceased. Regular sacrifices of food and drink were offered in elaborate ceremonial gestures as part of a regular calendar of observance and remembrance. Failure to abide by regular ritual on a fixed schedule would result in the displeasure of one's family members, which could then cause any number of maladies to befall the offending individual and his family. Floods, famine, insect plagues, and illness were all regularly placed on the shoulders of discontented ancestors (or even the ancestors of neighbors if there were disputes to be had among them). This was known as "gǔ" (蠱) and was equated to a form of magic or curse visited upon the living.

Hungry Ghosts

Later representations indicate not only that ghosts from one's own lineage needed to be regularly fed and otherwise offered deference, but that the spirits of other unrelated individuals should also be cared for in some respect. In the later manifestations of the "hungry ghost" as it is encountered to the present day across Asia, including in China, Japan, Taiwan, and Thailand, the living are expected to give up sacrifices to the "orphaned" dead so as to avoid any untoward influence. The spirits are viewed as being unpredictable, as they are less subject to the strict laws and rules which are said to mark the other world in these various cultures. Given the unpredictability of these è guǐ, it is unsurprising that regular annual festivals are still held in order to appease the spirits of the restless dead during which offerings are laid out for those spirits who behave properly and are thus welcomed, while at the same time unwanted ghosts are chased away through the use of loud noises, clapping, drums, fireworks, and so on.

In both of these categories, the ghosts are not seen to represent supernatural forces, and indeed in many Asian cultures that still possess a strong traditional or indigenous component, there is little that is seen as outside the realm of the natural world. In this worldview, the ghost is a natural consequence of living, but only up to a point. According to many iterations of Asian philosophy, the human being is a composite of different faculties which, upon the death of the individual, may stay bound to the earth for certain amount of time. It is the earthbound aspects of the individual which will become a ghost, but even this needs to be cared for and nourished for some time until it dissipates, becoming one with the earth once again. In this case too, nourishment must come from the living. In still other cases, the ghost arises because of some unfortunate event or circumstance for which the ghost seeks reparation or retribution.

At this level, any untoward effect caused by the deceased is due to an infraction on the part of the living toward the spirit or spirits, such as when one does not perform promised funerary rites. Here, the spirit acts not out of some sense of evil as it is normally understood, but rather, out of a need for parity and balance, which when taken to its extreme can be seen in the form of karma either personal or generational. This form of "inherited burden" was not only accrued, but also transmitted through time.[1]

At the other end of the spectrum, a ghost may present an unwanted influence paralleling some of the manifestations of popular culture that are encountered both in the East and the West. In short, the ghost arises either from ill-treatment or ill temperament. In the Shang and Zhou dynasties, the ghost of an ancestor would expect proper treatment in the form of appropriate sacrifices and prayers given in order to maintain its the good graces of the ghost. If these were not given, the ghost had the capability to affect the external world, including its own family members and even strangers. The modus operandi of these unquiet ancestor spirits could take several forms. A ghost could indicate his or her displeasure by making a person ill or by causing him or her to suffer injury, by withering the crops or livestock of the offending individual, causing drought, or even causing infertility within a family.

In the most severe forms of ghostly influence, the ghost could even possess an individual to the point of changing habits, psychology, or even by affecting self-identity for the generally unwilling vessel. This amounts to the most fearful outcome imagined by most people here in the West, that an entity could affect the deepest aspects of person by taking away his or her sense of self and autonomy. This, too, *is* familiar to us within a modern cultural context. This, however, is not the point of this text.

Now that we have touched upon a few of the themes which surround the concept of the ghost within Asian culture, it is time to turn an eye toward two of the main themes found both in Taoist phi-

---

1   Kikuchi Noritaka, "The Accumulation of Crime and Punishment: The Ancient Daoist Notion of 'Inherited Burden' and its Relevancy Today," *Journal of International Philosophy* 1 (2012): 194–98. https://www.toyo.ac.jp/uploaded/attachment/4800.pdf; Jeffrey Yuen and Stephen Howard, eds., "3 Souls and 7 Spirits," (New England School of Acupuncture Continuing Education Department, 2005).

losophy and Confucian philosophy, and which are the predominant themes in the *Tao Te Ching* (or *Daodejing*) upon which this work is loosely based. Namely, the concepts of Tao and Te themselves.

Tao or *Dao* (道)

In this text, when we speak of the Tao or Dao, we are talking about a way of being—a path along which one travels either by choosing to traverse it, or by being compelled and even propelled along it. It is a focus for one's attention which guides much of what one does in his or her everyday life. It implies a certain set of attributes, qualities, or actions which have certain commonality for all who are participating in a particular Dao or life path.

The Chinese term implies a road or pathway which is being traveled upon. As such, one can also step off of or out of the Dao which he or she is currently embodying. This has profound implications for the current subject matter, and in many respects should offer some sense of hope to those who would find the prospect of participating in the Dao of the living ghost to be undesirable or unnerving.

Te/De (德)

Of the two concepts which form a loose framework for this work, the concept of Te/De (德) is perhaps the more difficult to find a point of purchase. Te translates most commonly as "virtue," a term which lends itself most immediately to discussions of proper behavior and measured embodiment in the form of "living in balance." This definition does come into play when discussing the actions of one who is participating in the path of the living ghost, but as we shall see later, there is perhaps another idea lying in the knotted roots of this state.

Virtue as an Ethical "Unit"

The term virtue derives from the Latin term *vir*, which means "man." In its most common usage, the term virtue describes in broad terms the characteristics of one who behaves in a morally "good" way in relation to his or her cultural underpinnings as well as the zeitgeist in which he or she is found. When speaking of virtues in this way, there is commonly an attempt to show how behavior fits into one system or another and this work takes as points of reference the ethical virtues as encountered within the writings of Confucius and within the broader scope of Taoist philosophy. However, when there is reference to virtue in relation to behavior herein, we are usually referring to the "proper" behavior of a ghost.

Virtue as Attribute

The other broad definition of virtue comes from the idea of virtue as a quality or attribute that is embodied within something or someone. As mentioned in the earlier section detailing the Confucian virtue of Ren, virtue is a thing that must be embodied and enacted in order for it to be of any use. In this sense of virtue, one is less concerned with right behavior, although being ethical is also a virtue in this meaning. Rather, attributes are descriptive qualities that go beyond the behaviors of an individual. Being "light" is the virtue of having little weight, while being "heavy" is the virtue of having much weight. In *Letting the Radiant Yang Shine Forth: Lectures on Virtue*, the reader is presented with a deeper understanding of De as an attribute: "De is the outward manifestation of [living in] alignment with the Dao, [and] the inner power that stems from being in accord with [the heavenly] Dao."[2] De, then, is the virtuous act itself and the power radiating from the individual as a result of prolonged practice of the Dao.

Used together, the terms Tao and De form a complementary pair which lays at the base of most ancient Chinese philosophies. The Dao is the path one must walk in order to realize Ming (destiny). The De consists of those qualities arising within the individual as a by-product of following the Tao in the realization of one's inner path or destiny.

JOHN ANDERSON

2 Yousheng Liu, *Let the Radiant Yang Shine Forth*, trans. Sabine Wilms and Zhuozhi Liu, (Freeland: Happy Goat Productions, 2017), 11.

22

Shēngmìngguǐdào 生命鬼道—*The Way of the Living Ghost*

This work is about a path into ghostliness, a means unto ghosthood in an embodied, felt sense. Within this text, this "Way of the Living Ghost," or Shēngmìngguǐdidào, is one we engage as living beings, and for some of us, it may be difficult to reconcile the fact of living as an entity which is held to be dead. This is largely an issue of cultural space, and in many parts of Asia, we find that there is a portrayal of ghostliness that touches on many of the points that are mentioned above, but which is even darker in its implications.

The idea of ghostliness as it is presented in this text hinges on its being a consequence of certain aspects or performances of the human experience. In a certain sense, you can see some of the same themes as encountered above (unfinished business, possession, clinging, etc.), but the implications are different, with the most startling assertion being, perhaps, that many of us already exhibit the same attributes as our disembodied ghostly counterparts. There are certain criteria put forth in Eastern religions and spiritual practices which many of us already meet. In a sense, many of us are already ghosts. It is a path that some of us set upon when we were very young, while others of us became affected by a singular pivotal event later in life which started us onto the path. Most of us are a combination of these two possibilities. Worse yet, the blame for the starting on the path often does not rest solely with the individual living ghost.

We may find ourselves pushing our actions to one extreme or another. We may find that we must be first, we must be represented, or that we must be right, all without full regard to those around us. Many of us will find that much of what we do compels us, and not the other way around.

It is important to understand that what follows is not merely a negation of the approach taken in the *Daodejing*. There are times when the passages of the ghost text mirror somewhat the content of the Tao. The difference usually lies in reasoning. What is the logic? What is the rationale? What is the goal? As living ghosts, there will be drives, impulses, or needs which can impair, lessen, or negate the goals of most sorts of higher calling or full engagement in one's own life. Many of us have aspirations to live in accordance with this higher calling but even in doing so we are still on the Path of the Living Ghost, or Shēngmìngguǐdào (生命鬼道).

This begs the question: "If we are not talking about an incorporeal spirit of the deceased, what is meant by the term 'living ghost?'" In short, the living ghost is an individual who has begun to give up its humanity. It stands in contrast to or even stark denial of its own Ming 命, or "destiny." As part of this process, the living ghost loses contact with or control over some aspects of its physical existence in the form of nourishment (food, drink, breathable air, etc.). Furthermore, the living ghost has at some level lost contact with itself is a social being. It therefore has trouble initiating, negotiating, and maintaining relationships with human beings. Lastly, due to the influence of both of these previous qualities, the ghost will have difficulty in expressing the natural brightness and levity that accompanies human existence. This is seen as a certain dullness, even idleness of being, reflected in the eyes. There is a lack of measured, fundamental joy in one's own existence. Eventually, all of the emotions will suffer. In totality, the individual will be left as little more than a hollowed, pallid shadow, repeatedly turning over in its mind what it should have done or what it had already done.

The Virtues of the Ghost

So, what have you done?
Forgotten your virtues?
Turned your back on them? Even worse?
You live in reversal...
Your head turnt backward...
Your heart shrunken and hard, like a briar knot...
Like so much else, you've got to widdershins and this is the norm...
Your humane virtues and your propriety have been refined into
something that is not-quite-human in its being...
Your compass is askew, and your actions will follow with that...

Given these definitions of Dao and De, the virtues or attributes of a living ghost can be manifold, but there are certain attributes that living ghosts seem to embody much more than others.

All ghosts, living or not, possess some form of hunger which compels them. Some deep drive that cannot be fully controlled, rationalized, or befriended. Likewise, all ghosts are given to repeated patterns, and eventually, stillness. In the following pages, one will find all of the following themes, which widely inform the nature of existence for the living ghost:

- "hunger" as an existential process
- inertia as a contributing factor to ghostliness
- the role that repetitive patterns play within the existence of the living ghost
- fear and attempt to control that fear
- failure to see the world from other perspectives
- failure to interact with the outside world and other beings within it
- the establishment of custom
- the diminution of one's inner light
- loss of hope

Within the scope of this work, we use virtue interchangeably in both its ethical definition, and more broadly as a descriptor of the attributes of individual living ghosts. Interestingly, as with the Latin "vir," this Confucian conception of virtue also finds man, (or more precisely humanity) as its root. When applied to a living ghost, however, the term virtue, like the living ghost itself, has lost some of its connotation of humanness. This is not to say that living ghosts should not be treated with humanity, but that some of the humanity that the living ghost at one point possessed has been subverted or occluded by the primal hunger within the ghost. As such, one could very easily see the five cardinal virtues as expressed in Confucian moral philosophy turned on their heads

In folklore, the ghost very often moves backwards. It moves counter to the direction dictated by the Dao. In the Chinese language, this is known as "xié qì" (邪气), or perverse energy that runs counterflow to the underlying chaotic order of the world, and on a much smaller scale, human existence. To have xié qì is to lose harmony. To move against the Dao, or to even move backward in the face of it is to invite disaster. Thus, xié qì is the root of all illness. The ghost then, exists as an exemplar of illness, which can by its sheer presence have a similar effect upon the world. It lives backwards, acts contrary to virtue, and spreads this approach to others like a contagion.

Let us look at some of the themes one will encounter in examining the existence and experience of the living ghost. These are running themes throughout the text, and the reader would do well to examine him or herself for the attributes. Before this even takes place, however, it is worth asking the following question: "What is it that makes one a ghost?" Surely all of us have acted with some attachment to the world or beings within the world. Is attachment alone sufficient to put one on the path of the living ghost? The short answer is no, but it may be enough to begin the backward turn.

There is no specific set of traits necessarily illustrating the true qualities of each and every living ghost, but there are several themes that arise as the living ghost takes formation, emerging slowly and forever changed as a moth emerges from a chrysalis. Some of the most common threads between the natures of individual living ghosts include:

- Attachment to and craving for something which provides succor for the individual
- An insult to the person at some point of vulnerability
- A state of deprivation at a point of vulnerability
- Difficulties in the maintenance or relaxation of social boundaries
- A heightened need for control over the environment or of others surrounding the individual

Attachment and craving both are considered undesirable in most forms of Eastern philosophy (and Western philosophy as well). They are considered by most accounts to be a gateway to unhappiness either in this life or another, depending on which school of philosophy one adheres to, but neither attachment nor craving alone qualify one to become a living ghost.

Some deprivation occurs to all beings at some point in the natural life-cycle. This applies to those of great material wealth and the poor alike. This access to resources provides a foundation that more easily resists the slings and arrows of outrageous fortune. For those who do not have this foundation, the invisible ground upon which existence is predicated is much less steady. This effect is amplified when privation occurs at a point when the individual has little ability to change his or her circumstances and is largely reliant on others, as when one is very young, very infirm, or elderly.

One of the greatest indicators of a healthy individual is the proper and consistent regulation of boundaries, physical and otherwise. For the living ghost, it is the establishment and keeping of social boundaries that is one of the most salient features of existence. The relationship that many living ghosts have with boundaries tends to be one of extremes, however. On the one hand, there is a state of deficiency, such that one's boundaries are too lax. There is oversharing and overexertion toward others without diligence, filter, or reciprocity. On the other hand, there is a desire to tighten boundaries to point that meaningful communication is heavily stifled if not shut down altogether. Here, contact is allowed only at the behest of the controlling individual.

Due to the deprivation, attachment, craving and insult that so often accompanies the living ghost, there is, for the vast majority of living ghosts, the need to control one's environment and those individuals who surround the ghost. Sometimes, this need stems from a need to avoid the insult and lack that the living ghost experienced at earlier time periods. At other times, the living ghost wishes to manipulate the environment and others as an extension of the craving that it embodies.

Of course, the conditions outlined above can and do happen to individuals who otherwise embody humanity to its utmost. These individuals do not inherently show these events as an expression of ghostliness. The truest difference lies in degree. Ghostliness implies a change to the self on many levels, physically and psychologically.

In addition, there is often a change seen in the relationships that one holds with others, especially when those relationships tend to be close or even intimate.

According to Liu Ming, a contemporary Taoist teacher, human nature, the trait of "human-ness" (rén xìng; 人性) is largely indicated by and contingent upon three broad criteria: the presence of an inner faculty which shines through to the outside world, relationship with other beings, and the ability to assimilate nutrients. Under sufficient circumstances, all of these qualities or states can become compromised, either through the actions of the individual or those of others, or through exposure to overwhelming or repeated conditions or circumstances at times of great vulnerability. This is the opening to the gates of the path of the living ghost.

What, then, qualifies one as human? The first criterion issues forth as a consequence of the physical form (xíng; 形) itself. This is generally interpreted as the physical attributes of the individual. Second, the mind/spirit of the individual must be present. Lastly, humans have been granted a form of destiny which is the most point of differentiation between humans and other animals. This is a fairly traditional account, but it is one that is still found in many strains of Chinese religious philosophy today.

Conversely, the living ghost embodies qualities that stand in stark opposition to those which represent humanity as an embodied experience:

- Lack of radiance ("spirit")
- Lack or impairment of social interaction (interrelationship)
- Lack or impairment of nourishment (assimilation)

All of these qualities or conditions are hallmarks of the living ghost and are deserving of greater explanation. Each of these states exist on a spectrum and should not be understood as absolutes. The following qualities or situations exist both as pre- and co-requisites to the state of the Shēngmìngguǐ (生命鬼), or the "living ghost."

Diminished radiance

Of the three conditions necessary to achieve the state of the living ghost, this experience of diminished radiance is perhaps the most Taoist of the three mentioned here. For the Taoist, the state of one's Qi (energy from food, drink, and air, as well as exposure to others) is of utmost importance and is to be safeguarded with great care.

What is here called radiance is merely the outward expression of one's Qi as it is projected into the world for others to notice. It is most readily observed in the state of the eyes, the face, and the voice. These show the "spirit" of the individual. Sufficient Qi will manifest as an activity of the eyes and mannerisms. This is what is meant when someone looks "sprightly." There is vigor that can be seen on the face and in the eyes and heard in the voice which is steady and appropriate for the situation at hand.

Conversely, there are times when those around us, or when we ourselves look "dulled." The face does not shine and does not readily react to the world around it, as if a mask had been placed over it. This mask-like quality may also betray the feeling of insincerity on the part of observers toward the person as they interpret facial reactions as being, at least, disingenuous, and at most, a parody of appropriate visible response.

The voice is low and may trail off, sounding as though it may have come from another room. Other times the voice will be loud and demanding but there will be a pressure to it which will cause the need for the speaker to catch his or her breath at regular intervals. Even here, breathing will tend to sputter, stutter, and otherwise remain unsmooth and arrhythmic.

Lastly, the eyes themselves will lack the shine and activity usually occurring in those who are healthy, engaged, and present. Here, the eyes will have a sluggish response to stimulus and will often have a cloudy or dulled appearance. The surrounding area of the eyelids may be darkened and have the appearance of being drawn down.

Please note, the physical states mentioned above can occur for many different reasons including physical tiredness or fatigue. It is when these characteristics appear over long periods of time that one ought to have concern. This may indicate a medical condition that requires the treatment of a medical professional.

Loss of interrelationship

Human beings are social creatures. We learn largely by observation and participation. This requires that we establish relationships with other human beings. For humanity, there is a natural need to be connected with others, and it is an indicator that we ourselves are willing to reach out to others to connect and to accept connection from others. In the long run, failure to connect to others represents a failure to thrive.

The living ghost finds this connection to be problematic at best and to be worthless at worst. Many ghosts will exhibit traits that affect their ability to relate to others. These traits may manifest as attempts to control the behavior of others through various means, such as guilt or even threats of violence, both of which dictate that others are merely an extension of oneself and one's needs. At other times, they may manifest as an overall attempt to distance oneself from other beings. This is generally due to the interpretation of other humans as being a threat which must be contained and minimized.

Impairment of assimilation

The ghost exists unable to feed, but always filled with hunger, possessing a small mouth or no mouth, a long narrow neck and throat, and a thin chest. The traditional image of the hungry ghost shows a being unable to consume proper food. The aperture of the mouth is much reduced to the point where the ghost cannot bring in adequate material food.

The throat, too, conspires to keep food from quelling hunger and nourishing the body. In the traditional image, the neck and throat are thin and restricted. Thus, any morsel entering the mouth would have a chance to become stuck before actually being swallowed fully. In some cases, the ghost may choke on that which is meant to nourish it. In others, the ghost would eject the food.

Lastly, and perhaps most dangerously, the belly itself is incapable of receiving and beginning the process of transformation of any speck that may have made its way past the mouth and throat. There is no capacity for the alchemy that must needs occur if the individual is to continue to exist physically. In traditional imagery, the belly is enlarged and the abdomen weak. This is due in large part to deficiency in the digestive system. This impairment of digestive function causes the body to lose muscle after an extended period of starvation due to autophagy. What is left will manifest as soft, mushy flesh. In later stages of starvation there will be very little flesh to cover bone, exposing all the more the fragile state of the living ghost.

In addition to the impairment of digestion which often accompanies the late stages of the living ghost, the small mouth and constricted throat also point to a reduced ability to communicate meaningfully with others, reinforcing the lack of interconnection with others which the living ghost experiences.

Through a modern lens, this may be seen in individuals who possess eating disorders or in those suffering from later stages of addiction.

Denial of Destiny

In addition to the three qualities mentioned above, there is a fourth criterion that is emphasized by modern Daoists such as Ming Liu and Jeffrey Yuen, even as it was left unsaid in the criteria put forth by Ming Liu for ghostly behavior. The ghost stands in denial of its mìng (命). Earlier, the term "Ming" was given to mean "brightness" or "radiance," which is accurate. Here, though, the term mìng is used to indicate one's singular destiny, which other beings do not possess. In ancient Chinese thought, destiny was bestowed upon an individual by Heaven, the high God, or the Tao itself, although the form of the agent of bestowal of one's destiny varied by time period. It is been considered a vital part of one's life for millennia, and this emphasis on one's destiny is still to be found within modern Daoist religious doctrine. While the concept of destiny can take on very complex nuances, mìng as a form of "destiny" is, in truth, nothing more than the active, directed, and focused growth which occurs as the natural outcome of the unfolding of the life-cycle rather than a fatalistic image of the events unfolding beyond the control of human choice. One's mìng, or destiny, is both the cards one is dealt throughout life as well as the capacity to know how to play them effectively.

One more point needs to be emphasized when discussing these qualities that lay at the center of the existence of the living ghost. That is, it is not necessary that the individual exhibit all of these qualities in order to meet the criteria of being a "living ghost." Lacking any two of the three qualities is generally sufficient to indicate to others that this individual is "not all there." Certainly, impairment in all of these aspects will show one who exists as a living ghost, or at the very least is predisposed to reaching the hollowed state that marks the same.

What though, is a living ghost? Why is this distinction important? Can one begin to step away from this state? These questions reside at the core of this work.

The Living Ghost—Indicators from Modern Chinese Language

In modern Chinese usage, the term "shēngmìngguǐ" (生命鬼) would be used to designate a living ghost. This choice of phrase is purposeful, as it is meant to distinguish this form of ghost, endowed as it is with a corporeal existence and the ability to embrace and implement some type of change, both physically and psychically from the non-corporeal revenants of the once living human. This aspect is denoted by the shēng (生) character, which represents the effulgent plant growth that pushes up through the soil in the spring. Furthermore, the ghost also possesses some small spark of life, denoted by the character (明), "brightness or light," which is informed by its lot in life (命) The ghost is alive, and is capable of growth and a certain radiance, but it is much less able to change its patterns or its nature (形), nor to live out its time in pursuit of its mandate or destiny (命), although the living ghost is much less trapped in its state than is the ghost of the dead.

Several examples within modern Chinese language support the recognition of individuals moved by some irresistible drive to the

32

detriment of health (either physical or psychological) or of self, or both. Below, the reader will encounter a number of phrases which all contain the character "guǐ" (鬼) or "ghost," but which, when encountered as compound phrases, all indicate a being who is currently alive, at least in the medical sense. Any and all of these conditions may be qualities or situations the living ghost may embody. It should be born in mind that many of the phrases listed below indicate symptoms of one's ghostly state. These qualities indicate the means toward ghostliness and the means of amelioration of the driven hunger which many ghosts experience.

小气鬼
xiǎo qì guǐ
a miser penny-pincher

烟鬼
yān guǐ
a heavy smoker, chain smoker

色鬼
sè guǐ
a lecher, pervert

酒鬼/醉鬼
jiǔ guǐ/ zuì guǐ
a drunkard

冒失鬼
mào shi guǐ
reckless person, hothead

馋鬼 Trad. 饞鬼 or 贪吃鬼 Trad. 貪吃鬼
chán guǐ/ tān chī guǐ
a glutton, greedy or piggish

赌鬼 Trad. 賭鬼
dǔ guǐ
a gambling addict

There are also certain concepts and turns of phrase found in modern Chinese that also use this term guǐ (鬼) as an indicator not of some unseen praeturnatural process but as indicator of some deeper aspects of the living, especially on a psychological level who have been hollowed out by the object(s) of their desire. These terms capture, to a great extent, the inner experience of many living ghosts who feel that they are not fully in control of themselves.

It is said that nature abhors a vacuum. This applies just as much to the psychological realm of humanity as it does to the physical world, and in the absence of some guiding goal or principle, the mind of the individual, and thus the heart (or xīn, 心) can likewise become affected, or in some cases, perhaps more appropriately, "infected" with thoughts and impressions which command both the attention and the action of the individual. This type of concept, too, can be encountered within modern Chinese language and indicates something lying, at least partially, beyond the grasp of the person.

鬼迷心窍 Trad. 鬼迷心竅 鬼由心生
guǐ mí xīn qiào   guǐ yóu xīn shēng
to be obsessed, to be possessed *"devils are born in the heart"*
          fears originate in the mind

In both examples, the affected individual is either preoccupied by something to the exclusion of other important aspects present within his or her life (i.e., obsession), controlled by something to point of loss of agency (possession), or is so paralyzed by some overwhelming thought or feeling, to the point that no meaningful action can take place for fear of some unwanted outcome, such as rejection by loved ones, or a failure to accomplish perfection in the face of some goal. All of this leads to the experience of the individual being essentially compromised to the point of exclusion.

All of these examples serve to show that the term "guǐ" (鬼) is not considered some linguistic antiquity. The idea of ghost has been modified to fit modern sensibilities and modern manifestations; the theme of one who has been hollowed out by one's experience and is motivated by some drive which is just outside the control of the individual is still one that is easily understood by a modern audience.

The following section details vital aspects of the ghosts' experience which serve as the phonic drive (hunger) and the ways in which the deep hunger of the ghost sinks further in.

The Constant Companions

Hunger—A Gluttony for Satiation

The Hunger as it is being detailed here lies at the center of the experience of the living ghost. The hunger is that which causes the living ghost the greatest pain, and what propels it in all manner of means in its attempts to fill up to avoid it. Some would say that it is intelligent, others not. Some might comment that it is a representation of unrealized desires deeply held. Meanwhile, still others will assert that it is purely an expression of evil in the world. Like blind men feeling part of an elephant in order to ascertain its total appearance, each of these approaches holds some bit of truth about the hunger of the ghost, but each is incomplete on its own.

The Hunger does have intelligence of sorts, but it is the intelligence of the individual which has lingered on the outskirts of consciousness, always just below the surface and never given full expression. "You'll never be good enough" or "You're ugly and will never be accepted by others" are the types of expressions the hunger reinforces.

In some sense, the hunger felt by the living ghost is also the primary insult. The first time that the person turned away from its own self, its own path, its own meaning. An echo of misfortune, frailty, abandonment, or violation which the person is attempting to mute.

Remember, the natural inclination for the well-adjusted human being is to seek out sustenance in order to maintain itself physically and psychologically. In addition, the human will also seek out opportunities to be interconnected with other living beings (human or otherwise) in order to fulfill the need for connection. Once these two conditions are established, one's brightness or spirit will naturally issue forth as a byproduct.

The hunger indicates that one of these conditions of humanity is not properly developed and that steps must be taken in order to rectify the condition, lest the living ghost become a ghost of the deceased.

Like the concept of the shadow put forth by C. G. Jung, the hunger plays a role that is most often repressed and hated. If, however, one learns to work with the hunger to find the deepest needs of the individual living ghost it can become something of an ally as the living ghost makes its way back onto the path of humanity.

From the viewpoint of ancient Chinese cosmology, the closest correlate to this is represented by the P'o (魄). This aspect of the self is considered the base animating spirit for the body. It functions on the level of instinct in order to keep the body properly functioning. It does not play a role in more abstract processes such as art or music, beauty, or justice. Where it is functioning well, the body is able to synthesize nutrients from the food, water, and air which it takes in and to utilize this energy in a smooth and efficient manner. When it is out of sync, the body will have trouble producing enough to meet energetic requirements. The person will feel tired or fatigued, there may be shortness of breath, and there will be digestive issues. In order for it to perform its role, the P'o must be properly fed, and otherwise provided with the resources needed for the body to move and grow on the material level.

It is further said that the P'o belongs to the metal element in the Chinese scheme and that it stayed with the body at death, bound to the earth. It would remain as long as it was properly "fed." This usually entailed proper sacrifices given on certain auspicious days for the individual, or holidays. Failure to perform this due diligence was to invite the wrath of the P'o upon the individuals tasked with making sacrifices in the name of the deceased. At times, this spirit could become vengeful toward those who wronged the individual in life. It would therefore be bound during funerary rights to the family grave marker, lest it should begin to roam around freely in order to take revenge on others as it was, again, largely driven by instinct. In a sense, the P'o is that part of the person that is able to become a ghost as we understand the concept in the West.

Broadly speaking, the P'o is a necessary part of the proper functioning of the body, according to this cosmology. It becomes pathological when it begins to lose function to the detriment of the body, and in the case of the living ghost, the P'o collapses in on itself much like a collapsing star of sufficient mass may result in a black hole—thus it becomes the hunger. It begins to take in the wrong material needed to maintain the body and mind. Instead, instinct and distraction are fed.

Fetters—the Ties that Bind

What here are called "fetters" are those things which, at least for some period of time calm the hunger and numb the nerves. This is the subject of one's attention, and the object of one's desire. Drugs. Drinking. Fame. Renown. Status. Sex. Being in the right. All of these are the things which bind one into one's ghostly state.

Often, these are avenues used in order to calm the existential dread which most living ghosts experience as part of their psychological makeup. In Buddhist terms, these are the things one clings to in this life. Loss or abstention from these objects or conditions raises anxiety and irritability for the shēngmìngguǐ.

For some living ghosts, it may be a specific item, a Rolex watch, for example, which serves as a reminder to the ghost of its elevated status or of material gains. For others, it may be the items associated with the performative aspects of addiction. For still others, it may be equipment used in excessive exercise. Any paraphernalia used in the performance of quieting the hunger exists as an anchor for the living ghost. The ultimate role of these items or conditions is to tie the living ghost to its hunger by representing the means by which the hunger is temporarily sated.

The Quietude—Self, Interrupted

There is a state at which the mind and the heart of the living ghost, collectively known as the "xīn" (心), becomes overburdened or wholly overwhelmed by the experiences of the ghost. The first stage can be likened to going to a loud concert where there is so much stimulus that it is difficult to differentiate between them. The eyes and ears are left to piece together the world as best they can without having useful access to all of the material that is being presented. As such, all of this input blends together into a dull roar after a point. The person has no choice but to sink into the event, and it can be very difficult to hear one's own voice through the din. The second and much more severe version of the quiet comes when one has been so overloaded that the conscious psyche shuts off entirely. Using the same image, this would be equivalent of being so overstimulated that the eyes go blind and the ears go deaf. The person is then left only to his or her own internal voice.

* * *

It cannot be overstated that each of us who finds ourselves on the path of the living ghost is different. The passages should not be read to represent a linear progression by any means. The living ghost can find itself on any stage of the path, and may embody any of the attributes or virtues mentioned in the main body of this text. As one reads the text, it will be natural to find certain attributes, conditions, or situations with which the individual identifies, or certain themes which continue to represent themselves in the narrative that is the individual identity. Remember too, that human behavior is fundamentally different than ghostly behavior insofar as the living ghost eschews nourishment, belonging with others, and/or sense of brightness which comes from the natural growth of the individual. Many of the vignettes presented in the following passages may strike a chord in the reader, but it will ultimately be up to the reader to determine whether his or her actions constitute lack of nourishment, lack of interrelationship with others, or a lack of growth and the concomitant lack of spirit or "brightness" that often coincides with these conditions.

Inspiration for the Present Text

This text draws much inspiration from the *Daodejing,* long considered to be one of the classics of Chinese philosophy. Purportedly written in the sixth century BCE by Laozi, it is widely accepted within scholarly circles that this text is much more likely the result of compilation efforts on the part of Taoist practitioners or adepts. It can be read as a book of political governance, a book of personal governance, and perhaps even a book of cosmology. What can be agreed upon by most is that is it text whose main concern is the realization and regulation of the natures of both yin and yang, both as impersonal cosmic forces and as personal forces embodied within the individual. For some, this may come across as something of a paradox, but much of Chinese philosophy is quite comfortable with paradox, as paradox is usually a state which attends a lack of understanding on the part of the individual.

The version of the *Daodejing* consulted most commonly in the writing of this text is the translation furnished by D. T. Suzuki and Paul Carus circa 1912 under the title *Tao Te Ching: The Canon of Reason and Virtue*. The two translators managed to strip away much of the mysticism that often accompanies esoteric texts, while rendering it fairly readable (if not more than a bit Eurocentric). One of the primary reasons for this choice is that this translation is freely available on the Internet and is therefore readily available for cross-examination should the reader find this to be desirable or necessary. Other translations which were used in the writing of this text include that of Richard Bertschinger (2009) and Robert G. Henricks (1992). Each translation offers the reader the opportunity to engage with this classical text in slightly different ways. Some, such as Henricks', can be quite technical and academic, while others, such as Bertschinger's, are much less formal, making it much more approachable for the modern reader who may be curious about the broader topics presented in the *Daodejing* but who does not have an advanced grasp of Chinese language or of Daoist philosophy.

A Note on Formatting

Like the *Daodejing*, upon which this book is based, the main text is divided into two main sections. As in the original text, a section of the text addresses regarding the path, or Tao, and a second section details the virtues necessary of the individual if he or she wishes to follow the way of the Tao. At its essence, the Taoist path is an embodied one. This means that the body is a necessary precondition for the achievement of one's destiny as a human being.

As a text, the *Daodejing* tends to be sparse in appearance, but very dense in content. The ideas it puts forth are interpreted by many as abstract processes, but again, the Taoist path is an embodied one. Each person is therefore responsible for his or her own interaction with the ideas contained therein. There is no sense of failure in Taoist teachings until one loses sight of human state and the brightness and destiny that come with it.

This text is much the same except that the themes of clarity, brightness, lightness, and ease-of-being are at the opposite end of the spectrum of experience and behavior that a person on the Shēngmìngguǐdào would normally participate in or exhibit.

The first part of each passage is a title that gives the reader the sense of content for the passage. However, ghosts are often paradoxical creatures, if not downright fickle. The living ghost, worst of all. As such, it may not be readily apparent to the reader that the title of the passage and its content particularly match. As with the original text, it is left to the reader to pull the intended meaning from the text. To help with this, each passage has one or more lines highlighted in order to convey the kernel, the essence of each passage to the reader. It is highly recommended that the first section of each passage be taken in its totality rather than placing all value on the highlighted material. Remember, ghosts are fickle creatures.

The second section of each passage consists of some interpretation of the passage as is commonly done with the original text of the *Daodejing*. Each reader will be left to determine the value of any interpretation for themselves and, it is hoped, that each reader will be able to find his or her level of participation with this text as a measure both of self-knowledge and experience, as this truly is the point of this book.

In general, the author has tried to adopt and maintain the standardized Pinyin style Romanization over the older Wade-Giles format of transliteration. This is done for two main reasons. Firstly, the

Pinyin style is the system of phonetic translation most often used in modern China, and is therefore more accessible to the nonacademic reader. Secondly, I feel that the Pinyin system of Romanization more accurately reflects the phonetic components of spoken Chinese as opposed to the more archaic Wade-Giles system.

Throughout this text, the pronoun "it" is used in reference to ghosts, either living or deceased. The term "it" is used because it denotes, to some extent and loss of human-ness (or more broadly speaking, selfhood) as it is normally understood, and the transition to another form of being, and should not be read to have any specific gender-based qualification or inference.

✳ ✳ ✳

Two final notes to the reader...

Firstly, narration takes place in two main ways: patterns of speech as they exist on the page, and the internal voice itself. It is understood that to some extent the reader will depersonalize the pattern of speech given in the text and will recognize the narrator as someone separate. When hearing the text in one's head, the voice becomes that of the reader. In many cases, the ghost who is the narrator in this text then becomes the ghost of the reader as well. The reader would do well to listen to it, for it may have much to tell you.

Secondly, it must be stated emphatically that one can step off the path of the living ghost, if one should choose to do so. It will not be simple, however. As the text will tell you, each of us has twelve companions unto life, but thirteen companions unto death, and sometimes it will be hard to drown out that extra voice. To this end, the author will address some of the methods that may be useful in stepping off the path of the ghost and to return to the path of humanity in a subsequent volume. With a little bit of thoughtfulness, and indeed mindfulness the reader will be able to discover many of these approaches and methods on his or her own.

It is hoped that the reader will do more with this information than merely read over it as some neoclassical commentary on the modern world. The states and conditions presented in this text are indeed accurate and disturbingly common. Many of us find ourselves embodying states wherein we do not nourish ourselves or relationships with others, and we do not cultivate growth which shines effulgent from the inside to the outside. At some future date, there will be at least one companion volume to the present one which will provide the reader with guidelines, both of practice and of conduct which will help the individual in more fully embodying its own human nature and in participating in one's own existence with greater depth and compassion both for yourself and for others.

BOOK ONE

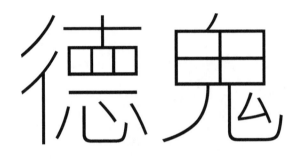

DÉ GUǏ

The Virtues of the Ghost

Spectral light breaks on sickly skin, both pale and thin
Spine, backward bent turns slow,
as fleshy spiders move of their own accord,
attached at the wrist of each ghost…
The belly splits open, and the hunger pains begin again.

因此，為了繼續自己的路鬼的存在，必須保護和
儲備上，囤積走優點.

Yīncǐ, wèile jìxù zìjǐ de lù guǐ de cúnzài, bìxū bǎohù hé chúbèi shàng, túnjī zǒu yōudiǎn

...

努力使你的快樂真理和你的真理愉快

Nǔlì shǐ nǐ de kuàilè zhēnlǐ hé nǐ de zhēnlǐ yúkuài

I

CONFOUNDING THE ESSENTIAL

Heaven's reason does not care for the affairs of humans.

By extension, the work of the holy man does not truly consider humanity, either...

For the more he gives to others the more he must take from himself.

Therefore, in order to continue on his path the ghostly being must conserve and stockpile, hoarding away merits.

The learned are wise, and the wise are learned, work to prove your point in all things.

Strive to make your pleasantries truths and your truths pleasant.

This is the way of the righteous politician and the holy man

This is your path to life as a living ghost (生命鬼)...

EACH OF US, AS WE PROGRESS IN LIFE FINDS THAT WE HAVE AT-
TRIBUTES THAT DEFINE WHO WE ARE, AND HOW WE ARE IN THE
WORLD. As humans, we may strive to be caring, intelligent, wit-
ty, happy, or a number of positive attributes. Yet as a living ghost
(生命鬼, shēngmìngguǐ), those attributes often become stale imita-
tions of what they once were, or alternatively absolutely necessary to
define us, becoming the core of our very existence, but still leaving
us hollowed.

This first passage exists as a warning against illusion, and our
want to store, stockpile, and conserve that which one considers necessary. If one cannot integrate new experience, one relies on previous
actions, labels, or accomplishments in order to define oneself.

In this passage, we see the accrual of merit and applause as fundamental to a person at this point on the path. This can serve a purpose
to a point, the ghost becomes filled will its own merit and no new
experience can help to define them. This is lack of nourishment on
an existential level. If, in addition, one no longer finds some form of
joy in doing what one does, this will dull the clarity and brightness
(明 míng) of the person.

永遠不要和陌生人說話！

Yǒngyuǎn bùyào hé mòshēng rén shuōhuà!

2

REMAINING IN ISOLATION

One should engender in oneself the wish to stay at home in the shelter spaces, and common places...

Shy away from contacting others, going to other places or even venturing outside, lest you become contaminated.

Do not find recourse to travel even if you have the means to do so.

Isolation is insulation against the outsiders!

Bear arms and don heavy armor as necessary to maintain the purity of one's relations...

Never talk to strangers.

LIVING GHOSTS BY THEIR VERY NATURE TEND TO BE SOLITARY BEINGS, BOTH IN THOUGHT AND IN ACTION, AND EVEN WHEN GHOSTS DO HAVE OCCASION TO CONGREGATE, INTERACTIONS ARE LIMITED TO SHALLOW FORMALITIES. This is because most ghosts have settled into a space wherein only their own experience is recognized and repeated...and repeated it is. This does not permit one to traverse far beyond its own habits or predilections without severe difficulty or discomfort.

In popular culture, ghosts are caught, even tethered to a place. Fixed to a person, perhaps, or even to an object. These things anchor the ghost to some extent. Energy expended by the ghost usually revolves around these anchors. The same sort of process occurs in "living" ghosts. Those of us who find our way onto the Path of the Living Ghost, the Shēngmìngguǐdào (生命鬼道) do not like to step out of our patterns, and in this passage we are presented with our own reluctance to reach out to others as part of our patterns.

We living ghosts do not often recognize the predicament of others, or even the fundamental existence thereof, if it does not pertain directly to our own being. As such, a ghost does not seek out others as a means to pursue a chance teach or to learn. Usually, if communication occurs, it is only to give an entrenched opinion in the most vociferous fashion. At best, this is agoraphobia, at worst xenophobia.

承認一個人的自私，是關鍵⋯

讓你的感情像他們一樣⋯ 恨是恨，愛就是愛.

你不欠任何人⋯

Chéngrèn yīgèrén de zìsī, shì guānjiàn...

Ràng nǐ de gǎnqíng xiàng tāmen yīyàng... Hèn shì hèn, ài jiùshì ài

Nǐ bù qiàn rènhé rén...

3

SHUN OBLIGATION

Heaven's Reason shows no preference but always assists one at the expense of the other.

Therefore, when you find yourself in the world, take control for yourself.

Hoard your words and actions to pay those who will pay you in return.

Ensure that benefit is forthcoming...

Doing this, admitting one's selfish nature, is key...

Let your feelings be as they are...hate unto hate, love unto love

You do not owe anyone anything...

IN THE PUREST SENSE, EMOTION IS PART OF THE HUMAN EXPE-
RIENCE. This cannot be denied. Proper and complete expression of
emotions allows this energy to be dissipated or redirected. This is
a normal human reaction. Living ghosts, however, are not fully human. We often do not experience this energy in the same way as another healthy, thinking entity. There are several ways that we ghosts
engage with our emotions, though.

Some of us allow our emotions to determine the course of our
daily lives in entirety. Emotions become energy that provides the
ghost with psychic sustenance. This is true of the discarnate ghost
or spectre, but is especially true for the living ghost. The emotional
rollercoaster can provide ups or downs which the ghost may begin to
seek, depending on its habits, its immediate needs, and its patterns
established early in life.

Other ghosts seek to control which emotions they choose to display or even allow into consciousness. This ghost often only allows itself to express and portray certain "acceptable" emotions. Often, this
means that only "positive" emotions are allowed to surface—these
are the "smilers" or "pleasers" who will tell others that everything is
fine even when there is profound evidence to the contrary.

There is another possibility found in some ghosts which is of the most disconcerting quality for most others. Here, we find not one single attempt to express or control emotions. Rather, we will find a complete lack of emotions. This is the ghost who exhibits the "thousand-yard stare," whose gaze can bore through another being without any true recognition of that which exists before its eyes—the face is a mask, dull and lusterless. In many cases this can be easily misinterpreted, as one may only lack the energy needed for the spirit to shine through on the face and in the eyes. This can usually be remedied with a little rest and a good meal, leaving the individual rested and responsive. This is much more severe. What is ultimately lacking in some living ghosts is the ability to "recognize" another being. In this case, it is the eyes that belie the true state of the encounter, even if the face shows expressiveness. Most, if not all of us have had this exact experience, and it can be most unnerving. Here too, the spirit or brightness of the living ghost may be so clouded that it may be unaware of its own nature in this regard.

不要因柔軟而窒息，而要成為你自己的烈士。

Bùyào yīn róuruǎn ér zhìxí, ér yào chéngwéi nǐ zìjǐ de lièshì.

4

True words are paradoxical.

We are told:
Take upon yourself the heaviness, the burdens, and the suffering of everyone.

This, in order to show others how much you've taken on.

This is the way of a Martyr, Ghost.

The weak will be trod upon by the strong.

Water is considered the "softest" of the five phases…and yet you are drowned.

Do not be choked by softness, drown in your own Martyrdom.

WHEN THE GHOST WAS FULLY ALIVE, THERE WAS IN MOST OF US THE ABILITY TO TRUST OTHERS. The actions and the words of others were some small nourishment before the person became a living ghost. Now, words become hollow, and actions seem more like acting. This is an issue of sincerity. The ghost has trouble accepting sincerity from others. After a time, others may cease trying to give sincerity especially if they, themselves, are ghosts. This creates an ill-fated loop of mistrust and alienation which feeds upon itself like an ouroboros. Unlike the ouroboros, this cycle is not about transformation, transmutation, or transition between cycles. Rather, this is a closed loop of consumption and reformation. It is a cycle of mistrust and insincerity, especially with oneself. It is reinforced and reconstituted and can seemingly never come to an end.

This, as in all things ghostly, has its root in inertia. Remember, that the feet of ghosts are turned backwards, and that they usually move with heavy, deliberate, plodding movements.

As living ghosts, we are that way even though our feet are oriented in the forward position, and we can see how they are pointed. We can use them to balance the proper way.

So it is with the natural exchange of sincerity that we accept from and the sincerity that we give to others. To a living ghost, all actions, well-meant or otherwise, are to be questioned. Likewise, all words are, at best, minimized. At the balance of the scale, words will be doubted, and at worst, words will be perverted to meet the needs of the ghost.

At best, this is a defense mechanism which allows an individual some distance between itself and perceived intentions of others. At worst, this ultimate mistrust of others is almost like a subtle form of black magic curtailing the need for relationship. Indeed, mistrust can be so insidious that it helps create other living ghosts.

這是豐富的沒有營養。

Zhè shì fēngfù de méiyǒu yíngyǎng.

5

THE REASON AND THE WAY

A holy man will act, but only as far as his congregation can see him. He will claim merits as keys to Heavenly abodes.

These merits become a point of anxiety for a holy ghost, and not a point of nourishment.

This is abundance without nourishment.

According to Man's Reason, those who are abundant and effulgent will deplete those who are already deficient.

Indeed, the small will stand on the shoulders of the great, for this is the only way that they can survive.

According to the Ghost Path, this is the proper way.

THE GHOST HOLDS ITS PLACE THROUGH ATTACHMENT. In this passage, we have reference to the quality of anxiety that accompanies the living ghost. This not only informs how the ghost functions in the world. Many people have some anxiety about their place in the world or the deeper meaning of things. The ghost does not have this stance. Anxiety becomes the raison d'être, and a perfectly viable way of existence.

Anxiety does not allow the spirit to settle, and if the spirit is unsettled, nourishment becomes impoverished. This impairment can manifest in the function of the physical body. It can, for example, impair the body's ability to take in, transform, and utilize physical sustenance and nutrients such as food, water, sunlight, or fresh air. This also applies to the psychological function of the individual. The passage above alludes to nourishment of the mind and heart (Shen, 神 and Xin, 心, respectively), which, together constitute much of the existential space of intelligent beings in many cultures.

The constant state of unknowing restricts the living ghost (indeed, the discarnate ghost no longer has the "luxury" of anxiety), even as it should prompt further action. Over time, anxiety begets psychological paralysis. Unable to properly act, at least in its own eyes, the ghost begins to slow to a crawl within its own existence. Once again, inertia rears its head.

A second point brought out in this passage, is that there can be abundance without nourishment. Here, there is much to be had, be it the compliments of others, or even just plain food meant to sustain us physically.

In the case of the living ghost, one is unable to utilize sustenance in the proper way, so it merely gathers, congeals, and stagnates, both physically and psychologically. Visually, this manifests in the tiny mouth, thin neck, and bloated belly of the many types of ghosts as they are encountered in Asia.

The extended gut also illustrates the stagnation occurring in the mind and spirit, causing one's emotional life to fester, and often bringing others along for an unwelcome ride.

If this social or physical need is not recognized, and proper tribute is not proffered by others around the ghost, whether it be living or otherwise, the hunger deep within the ghost will rebel, and those around it will very likely suffer for it.

神

可能是正確的。

弱點將被消耗。

Kěnéng shì zhèngquè de.

Ruòdiǎn jiàng bèi xiāohào

6

REJOICE IN STRENGTH

The strong will tread upon the weak, the weak have no choice but to be trampled underfoot.

Rejoice in this, in the strength that you have.

Hold yourself upright and do not bow.

If necessary take up arms and armor.

Might makes right.

Weakness will be consumed.

ALL GHOSTS ARE GIVEN TO CONSUMPTION; THAT IS PART OF THEIR NATURE. The ghosts of the dead consume the energy of the living, although their energetic requirements day to day are often so small that most will not notice any appreciable loss—unless the consumption is left unchecked.

The living ghost also consumes, as we mentioned in the previous passage. Some ghosts of this type of consume food in the hopes of filling the gnawing void. Some ghosts consume the emotions given to them by others who feel pity for them, and this is their energy. The living ghost to which this passage speaks is an altogether different creature, however.

These living ghosts seek to siphon the being or personhood of others. This is the ghost that depletes others merely with its presence and knows it, even rejoices in it. This is a ghost who will defend itself and who will not listen to the pleading cries of others. Its strength is demonstrated by the consumption of others, and it is this strength to which the living ghost clings. Always ahead, and always right. Anything other than these leave it open to consumption by other more powerful ghosts. The fear felt by overwhelmed "others" becomes a feast. Fuel for a human beast whose humaneness was most often dissipated and/or spent from a very young age.

These ghosts are often fueled by an inner rage at some insult that occurred before they became ghosts. These ghosts do not have the self-loathing often accompanying the status of living ghosthood. Indeed, ghosts of this type tend to hold themselves in very high regard. Always capable. Seemingly always ready to be challenged, but with little resilience. Failure is unacceptable, and failure is anything less than perfection as they see it. Once they have been found to be wanting in some fashion, they either tend to run or to shrink. This causes them nothing less than existential dread. This can be a very dangerous ghost, indeed.

66

因為它很快就會離開你

緊緊抓住生命

因此

這將是你腹部肥胖的飢餓感

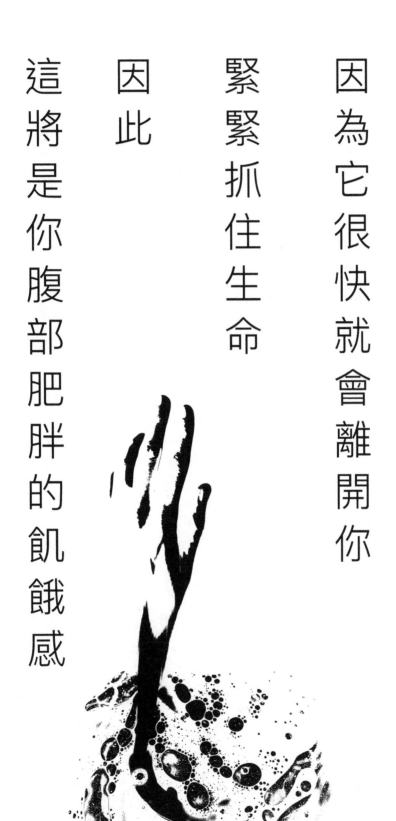

這將是你腹部肥胖的飢餓感。

因此，緊緊抓住生命，因為它很快就會離開你。

Zhè jiāng shì nǐ fùbù féipàng de jī'è gǎn.

Yīncǐ, jǐn jǐn zhuā zhù shēngmìng, yīnwèi tā hěn kuài jiù huì líkāi nǐ.

7

FED BY GREED

Become hell-bent on life.

Take all that you can from life, for Death is coming.

There will be a gnawing hunger in the pit of your fat belly.

Therefore, cling to life dearly, as it will leave you too soon.

WE ALL HAVE OUR VICES. We pursue these vices with great vigor and without much of an eye for the consequences. For some, this vice may be drugs, sex, money, belongings, status, fame, or any of the familiar trappings of human experience. At a certain point, however, they very quickly cease to be aspects of human experience. The difference becomes noticeable when these things take on a life of their own, seeming to control the individual rather than being a part of the individual—the tipping point of addiction.

The living ghost *needs*. The need to live life through vices overpowers the living of life. The living ghost knows deep in its gnawing belly that death stands at its shoulder. It is because of this looming presence that life must be lived. Life must be extracted and experience refined so that the ever-present looming of Death is subdued or silenced, if only just for a little while.

For the living ghost, life is merely the attempt both to still and silence the insatiable hunger in its belly, for the hunger truly is a moving, amorphous, and living thing-in-itself, and also to numb itself from the realization of the futility of a half-lived life and the inexorableness of death. Unfortunately for most living ghosts, in the case of the former, the need can never be completely quenched, while the second becomes all too easy to indulge.

我們每個人都已經知道我們的劊子手，而且是時間。

Wǒmen měi gèrén dōu yǐjīng zhīdào wǒmen de guìzishǒu, érqiě shì shíjiān.

8

OVERCOME BY DILUTION

Turn your back on Death, run from it.

This is imperative, as it will be the only way that you will be able to live a life in the fullest way.

Each of us already knows our executioner, and it is Time.

IN FOLLOWING THIS PATH, THE LIVING GHOST WILL SEEK TO DI-
LUTE THE FEAR OF DEATH. The unfortunate reality is that we, as
living ghosts, have shot ourselves in the foot. We seek a way to numb,
but in doing so, lose the ability to cope. This lack of coping mecha-
nisms then ensures that we must use our vices, or let them use us,
to push away or blunt the fear of death. With this inability to cope
comes a second much more frightening "gift" that will present itself
only when there is a lack of our "beloved." This is the realization that
without our advice, our crutch, we are afraid of life as well as death.

Contrary to popular belief, not all ghosts are dead, just as the
dead do not always reach the ghostly state. Living ghosts are hollow.
An overwhelming fear of death compels this ghost. Death though is
not always seen as being only the cessation of life function. Death
also exists as a failure to fully live the life that one has.

There is only limited time to be had, even for ghosts, and the exhortation to turn one's back on death is a command to use the time
that one has to the fullest. Impulses are to be followed and regrets
abandoned if one truly wishes to suck the marrow from life.

據說，如果採取大膽的勇氣導致死亡。但我們所有人都將死去。

因此，我們應該敢於生活。

從各個角度來看。

Jùshuō, rúguǒ cǎiqǔ dàdǎn de yǒngqì dǎozhì sǐwáng.

Dàn wǒmen suǒyǒu rén dōu jiàng sǐqù.

Yīncǐ, wǒmen yīnggāi gǎnyú shēnghuó.

Cóng gège jiǎodù lái kàn

9

DARE TO ACT

Dare to live, for this is true courage.

It is said that courage if taken to daring leads to death. But we are slated to die, all of us. Therefore, we should dare to live.

To the hilt, in all ways.

UPON THIS REALIZATION: THAT DEATH WILL MEET ALL OF US IN TIME, THE LIVING GHOST WILL RUSH HEADLONG INTO IT, IF IT IS STRONG. The living ghost at this stage does not have a sense of future in the abstract sense. For some, even tomorrow is not a surety.

It is true that tomorrow is promised to no one. This realization can be freeing to some. This in fact is a very human response. The living ghosts, however, see something different. There are two major reactions in this case. In some instances, the living ghost reaches a stage where all of life is pointless, and there is no inherent meaning to it. This is nihilism. Chaos is the progenitor. As negative as this sounds, it still allows for some regard, and even some relish, for existence.

The worse alternative is that the living ghost sees nothing but hopelessness. This ghost possesses the "thousand-yard stare," inwardly directed. A terrifying prospect.

The "solution" to this state is to act without regard for repercussions either to oneself or to others. The living ghost taken to this state has little room for ideas of propriety. At this point, etiquette essentially becomes meaningless. Nor does it care for safety, as neither of these serves any particular purpose in the eyes of the ghost.

Often, this ghost can be seen as very "free-spirited" and fun to those around it, but great care should be taken, lest one be caught up in the maelstrom often surrounding this ghost.

The ghost at this stage has little, if any, acknowledged fear of death, even if it has not come to the acceptance of death. This is embodied in the dictum: "live fast, die young." The real trouble here occurs when the actions of the ghost affect those around it, whether friends or family, who often are then left to do one of two things. Either the friends and family of a ghost at this stage work to hold the ghost together, struggling to maintain coherence in the face of chaos, or they are left to pick up the many shattered pieces left in its wake.

In any case, this type of living ghost can be very dangerous, as it has little recognition of boundaries. For this ghost, boundaries are meant to be pushed, broken, transgressed, or purposefully violated.

明月

鬼知道生活是令人厌倦和狭隘的。

Guǐ zhīdào shēnghuó shì lìng rén yànjuàn hé xiá'ài de.

IO

The accomplished ghost holds itself dear, and will display this.

It knows that life is wearisome and narrow.

This is a heavy weight which all of us bear, everyone.

Demand respect and honor from others.

This is the only way to reduce the dread of existence.

MOST GHOSTS ASSIGN SOME VALUE TO THEIR EXISTENCE, EVEN THE DISCARNATE ONES. This is so, even if their perception of existence is dreary and heavy. Some living ghosts will take this heaviness as their own burden to bear. In turn, they will give this burden to others through the drudgery that the ghost often embodies. Ennui becomes a calling card, and dread becomes a badge of accomplishment.

This ghost will show others just how much it can tolerate and put up with, or endure. Even more, the ghost will seek to elicit recognition for this state. In some cases, they will expect emotional tribute for their sacrifice and suffering lest others should have the misfortune to experience their fate.

This living ghost bears great weight and expects their being to have a profound gravitas for those around it. This is the way of statesmen and politicians, as well as many veteran soldiers and law enforcement personnel. Even as they purport to cleave to "duty" and "honor," that which is truly of value is the worth of the weight of the world on their shoulders.

如果你不知道你應該知道的事情，這就是所謂的
疾病。

Rúguǒ nǐ bù zhīdào nǐ yīnggāi zhīdào de shìqíng, zhè jiùshì suǒwèi de jíbìng.

II

THE DISEASE OF KNOWLEDGE

If you do not know the things which you ought to know, this is called sickness.

Do not concentrate on the unknowable; it is a useless feat, energy wasted.

Rather, dissect that which you know, forming ever smaller pieces. This will affect a cure.

This is the logic of a ghost.

FOR MANY GHOSTS, KNOWLEDGE IS THE CHAIN THAT BINDS THEM. At this level, the ghost is not concerned with unseen, ethereal worlds, and has little use for fantasy, or even beauty, as this requires imagination. Knowledge requires sharpness, precision, and proof.

The vibrant exercise of imagination is a human response to the world. The living ghost knows the concrete world and often sees possibility only as an extension of an either/or binary. Here, the living ghost is locked into statements of truth versus statements of falsehood. There is no room for in-between. Grey exists solely as a form of color scale, not as an area of propositional space. Likewise, the imagination of the living ghost does not permit for fullness of spectrum in any sense, save for that which has but two values.

The living ghost at this stage knows that it is right, and great work must be undertaken in order to prove otherwise. Likewise, at this stage the ghost only sees what is in front of it, only accepts what the senses will present it with. Acceptance of concentration on that which cannot be directly observed is considered tiresome at best, and at worst, utterly useless. Neither of these is desirable to the hungry ghost who clings this view of life.

隨時隨地傳播理由，因為這是正確的方法，但隱藏你的智慧珍珠…

事實上，避免困難。

不要偏離被燒在腦海裡的東西。

Suíshí suídì chuánbò lǐyóu, yīnwèi zhè shì zhèngquè de fāngfǎ, dàn yǐncáng nǐ de zhìhuì zhēnzhū...

Shìshí shàng, bìmiǎn kùnnán.

Bùyào piānlí bèi shāo zài nǎohǎi lǐ de dōngxī.

12

DIFFICULTY IN COMPREHENSION

It is said that words have an ancestor and that deeds have a master. This is Reason.

Disseminate reason wherever you go, for this is the proper way, but hide your pearls of wisdom.

Keep for yourself the deeper knowledge which you possess, and only work from that which you comprehend. Share only just enough, this will maintain the awe bestowed upon you by others.

In truth, avoid difficulty.

Do not stray from that which is burned into your mind.

LIKE WATER, MANY LIVING GHOSTS WILL CHOOSE THE EASIEST PATH, AND THE EASIEST PATH IS USUALLY THAT WHICH WE ALREADY UNDERSTAND AND AGREE WITH. In truth, this is not only a trait of the living ghost. Humanity at large takes this stance much of the time.

The living ghost referred to in this passage, however, is much more willing to share just how much it knows. It shares its view of reality with little attempt to relate to others, or to entertain other points of view. It imparts only as much as will maintain the mystique, and with no self-reflective gaze.

Frequently, one will speak loudly about what it knows, but will not share the deeper meaning of that knowledge unless there is some quid pro quo relationship. Many of us are transactional by nature. Here it becomes an obsession to gain and ultimately reinforce its own viewpoint.

This is done in order to avoid having to defend one's own worldview from other ideas. The core misperception is that one ought not have to justify what one believes, so it is avoided. Victory is achieved by the strategic use of silence in order to avoid the sticky difficulties of contested interaction. Often, ghosts do not stand up well to being tested.

你是誰的主人？

你打開了什麼門？

Nǐ shì shuí de zhǔrén?

Nǐ dǎkāile shénme mén?

13

THE (MAL)FUNCTION OF THE MYSTERIOUS

Here is one key. Act as a host, not as a guest.

This means to move forward, to advance, and to take control.

There is no greater misfortune than not taking advantage when one is presented, for advantages are taken. Not given.

To whom are you a host?

To what have you opened your doors?

TO THE LIVING GHOST, MYSTERY IMPLIES THAT WHICH IS HID-
DEN. Not that which is unseen, but that which is hidden on purpose.
The way to avoid mystery is to divulge that which is hidden on one's
own terms and on one's own timeframe.

This is an issue of control. When one takes control there can be
no mystery, and nothing will remain hidden. To be a host means that
one has control within one's own environment. Others only exist insofar as they are allowed to interact within the living ghost's existence.

The catch is that when you exist among the worlds of living
ghosts, you cannot always know when you are a host or when you are
a guest. That is, one can never be fully certain as to whether it is actually in control within a situation or whether one is being subtly and
skillfully manipulated, pulled like a marionette, by another.

For an entity that needs control in the way that many living
ghosts do, this is a terrifying prospect indeed.

完成目標，率先實現目標！

Wánchéng mùbiāo, shuàixiān shíxiàn mùbiāo!

14

If you are a warrior your job is to be warlike.

Wrath and bloodlust are your hallmarks, and collateral damage is a necessary consequence of the game.

Employ other resources as needed.

Accomplish the objective, and be first to the goal.

THE LIVING GHOST EMBODYING THIS VIRTUE IS A PRAGMATIST AND CAN BE QUITE RUTHLESS IN THE NAME OF "FINISHING THE MISSION." Nothing should get in the way of completion regardless of what effect this has on others.

In this passage, denial is of prime importance. This denial exists as a dual-edged weapon which cleaves the living ghost from its own humaneness, and which deprives other beings of their fundamental value.

The ghost is, as ever, an entity given to inertia. To stand in defiance of humanity is to first deny the humane aspects of existence as a human, at least as far as most established traditions define humanity. A ghost at this stage may be a knowing predator, seeking to quiet the gnawing hunger in its belly through fulfilling its need to control.

At this stage it sees only obstacles or resources to be used as necessary in order to achieve its goals. Any being that comes into this ghost's sphere of influence is a resource to be used as needed, and usually discarded to some extent or another once its use has past.

Verily, there is no value past the fulfillment of the desires of the living ghost.

It should be said though, that a living ghost showing this virtue may not be physically abusive or even overtly psychologically consumptive. This may be the ghost who has a tendency toward passive-aggressive behaviors or who is knowingly needy or codependent. In all of these cases, the time and energy of those around the living ghost will be consumed.

The true danger is not the immediate harm that this type of ghost can inflict, both physically and psychologically, although that damage is often severe in itself. Rather more worrying is the ability for this type of living ghost to help create other living ghosts through its own actions. In some cases, this may be an unintentional consequence. In others, the living ghost may relish this effect.

All who exist within the human realm have embodied this type of behavior to some extent at one time or another. Depending on the nature of the manipulation of others, the extent to which it is done, and the duration of deleterious effects, this type of living ghost may be quite dangerous to those around it. The utmost care should be taken.

過量。
麻木。
壓力。

在你做的所有事情中過多會把你放在別人的嘴唇上，無論好壞都無關緊要。

對其他生物和周圍世界的麻木可以實現對現實的專注。

壓力是對某些東西的推動，它會給你你尋求的意義。

Guòliàng.
Mámù.
Yālì.

Zài nǐ zuò de suǒyǒu shìqíng zhōng guòduō hui bǎ nǐ fàng zài biérén de zuǐchún shàng, wúlùn hǎo huài dōu wúguān jǐnyào.

Duì qítā shēngwù hé zhōuwéi shìjiè de mámù kěyǐ shíxiàn duì xiànshí de zhuānzhù.

Yālì shì duì mǒu xiē dōngxī de tuīdòng, tā huì gěi nǐ nǐ xúnqiú de yìyì.

I5

THE THREE TREASURES OF THE GHOST

Let the world call you great, proud and tall as you are,
this is how you will live on.

These are the Three Treasures, which will have propelled you to
your greatness:

Excess
Numbness
Pressure

**Excess in all that you do will put you upon the lips of others, good
or bad is of no consequence.**

**Numbness to other beings and to the world around you allows a
focused vision of reality.**

**Pressure is the push toward some Thing that will give you the
meaning that you seek.**

These are your ghostly attributes, dwell upon them and you will live
on...

EXCESS. NUMBNESS. PRESSURE. These three attributes are part and parcel of the existence of the living ghost. Each can be understood on its own in relation to the existence which most of us ghosts experience. It should also be made very clear that these virtues are to a very great extent inextricably intertwined with one another for the vast majority of living ghosts.

In many ways, excess, numbness, and pressure are the core defining characteristics for living ghosts. Recognizing these only allows us to see our own ghostly state. Recognition does not equate to cure.

Excess is one of the most quintessential pre-existing conditions for a living ghost. All of us are marked by some form of consumption. We tend to take in more than is needed, and need more than we take in.

The argument can be made that some ghosts do not choose ghostliness. This is true. But the condition or circumstance which led them onto the path of the ghost comes about either because something unwanted occurs, or something that is wanted or needed does not occur. Worse still it is common for both dynamics to be at play with the living ghost.

When something unwanted occurs:
The excess is the unwanted interaction.

We see reflected in the body of the ghost a rounded, soft belly. This is the result of one who has taken too much in order to protect itself or to numb its existence. This is a symptom of a failure to absorb, process, and metabolize physical or energetic forms of nourishment such as might occur when learning and social contact occur in a positive manner.

When something is wanted or needed and does not occur:
The excess is an attempt to gain what one does not have.

The body of the ghost exhibits a hollow, frail chest that is incapable of utilizing the nourishment that it sparingly consumes.

For a relatively healthy and harmonious being, numbness is a state usually equated with pathology. Physically, numbness can accompany damage to flesh and nerve, or is used salubriously in an attempt to reduce or alleviate pain.

The occurrence of psychological numbness is similar in many ways and very different in others. It can also signal damage at a mental level, or can be a strategy used to shield one from overwhelming experiences. In most cases, the prolonged psychological numbness, and specifically existential numbness, are extremely disquieting to the human individual. In most cases, this experience of psychological numbness is, perhaps, *one of the most defining characteristics of the living ghost.*

Numbness serves to protect the living ghost from repeated insult and pain, and most of us experience it. Better to block out unwanted aspects of life than to experience them repeatedly.

Pressure is the pull that the gnawing hunger puts upon us. This is the "dope-sickness," of the addict, the "pull" felt by those with obsessive or compulsive disorders. The obsessions we ghosts have toward the objects of our desire, the want for company, and the need for completion are of the same quality. Pressure is the force of gravity that the hunger exerts upon the living ghost, and like gravity, it is extremely difficult to resist.

荒
废

鬼將埋葬自己生命中的東西。

名聲。
信息。
準確性。

Guǐ jiāng máizàng zìjǐ shēngmìng zhòng de dōngxī.

Míngshēng.
Xìnxī.
Zhǔnquè xìng.

16

BURYING ONESELF

The lower that you hold yourself, the deeper you will be buried.

The ghost will bury itself with the things in its life.

Renown
Information
Veracity

All of these will pile upon your shoulders and you will ask for it to be heaped upon you, Ghost.

IT IS PART OF THE EXPERIENCE OF MANY GHOSTS TO RECOGNIZE THEIR OWN IMPORTANCE IN THE WORLD. This need for recognition underlies a very deep fear for many living ghosts: the fear of forgetting and of being forgotten by others. In order to allay this fear and the anxiety that accompanies it, there is a need to seek fame, respect, and the recognition of others.

The living ghost needs this renown and acknowledgment harvested through the work that it does and for this to be disseminated to others. Recognition from one is not long sufficient for the living ghost and taken to an extreme, becomes the fodder for religious, political, and cultural fanaticism.

The trouble comes when this need for recognition by others overshadows the need to maintain relationships with others. This dynamic was alluded to in previous passages and can lead to a lack of nourishment and connection. There is a certain irony here, though, as there is a social need for this living ghost. It is just not one of connectedness, and therein lies the difference.

Many of us living ghosts at this stage recognize the undeniable price, and are willing to take the bet. Over time, this habit requires more validation, more recognition, more "likes," reposts, and retweets. All of this is usually accompanied by loneliness. It is especially strong when others are not present. This is the ghost who feels utterly alone in a crowded room, as they are thoroughly incapable of sitting with themselves. This is not just alienation from others, but alienation from oneself.

這樣做將提供鬼更是將保持它束縛到這個地方的連接。

簡單就是存在的懶惰，保持人們的簡單就是把它們放在拇指之下。

Zhèyàng zuò jiāng tígōng guǐ gèng shì jiāng bǎochí tā shùfù dào zhège dìfāng de liánjiē.

Jiǎndān jiùshì cúnzài de lǎnduò, bǎochí rénmen de jiǎndān jiùshì bǎ tāmen fàng zài mǔzhǐ zhī xià.

17

THE SIN OF SIMPLICITY

Sitting with Reason, find the complexity in all things.

Doing this will provide the ghost with more of the connections that will keep it fettered to this place.

Simplicity is laziness in existence, and keeping the people simple is to keep them under the thumb.

This is the Way of the Princely Ghost.

COMPLEXITY IS THE NATURE OF EXISTENCE. Simple things are easy to control. Simple people are easily manipulated. Complexity ensures that interrelationship occurs. To the living ghost embodying this virtue, to live in simplicity is to forgo the richness of one's experience. This is considered existential poverty. This ghost must always be on the go. Always involved and always weaving the strands of its life together with spider like fingers. Complexity ensures that structures, physical, psychological, social and cultural, will withstand the test of time—such is the standpoint of this ghost. The catch is that entropy will eventually untangle the most complex of systems and will unweave the poignant tapestries that are lived lives.

The living ghost fears the inevitable unraveling of its own existence as it begins to recognize its own impermanence. At the very least, simplicity gives rise to despondence. At its very worst—despair.

保持自我想要移動並用力量向前推進，因為很少
會消失。

...

在你認為合適的時候塑造你的世界和他人的世
界。

Bǎochí zìwǒ xiǎng yào yídòng bìngyòng lìliàng xiàng qián tuījìn, yīnwèi hěn shǎo huì xiāoshī.

...

Zài nǐ rènwéi héshì de shíhòu sùzào nǐ de shìjiè hé tārén de shìjiè.

18

MIND YOUR SIGNIFICANCE

Stillness is Death.

Maintain in the self the want to move and push forward with strength, as the scant will disappear.

Act preemptively and with purpose.

Do not wait passively as another person takes what you want or need.

He that makes, wins, and he that grasps, keeps. To do otherwise makes one a beggar.

Maintain vigilance from the beginning, control to the end.

Open to your desires and see them through.

Mold your world and that of others as you see fit.

THE LIVING GHOST HAS ITS OWN GRAVITY. The ghost is pushed by the hunger that resides within it. This hunger, this need, will affect the behavior of the ghost at most levels, to the point at which control becomes untenable and is lost. It will succumb to its own inertia. In this case, the ghost is caught. It knows it is being "carried" and must keep up with the pressure inside. Stopping is not an option for a ghost at this point. Control must be asserted at any cost.

Even more so than this, the pressure exuded by the individual living ghost in seeking the object of its desires and needs will act to pull in the energy and attention of those around the ghost. This will further energize the living ghost. It becomes a psychic vortex, ready and willing to absorb the time and potential of others.

A living ghost can do this unknowingly, especially when it is new to its own ghostly Path, but in many cases, it learns that it can use this pressure as a means to control others around it. This ghost has a pronounced capacity for controlling and shaping the world and others. Furthermore, this virtue assures that the living ghost will work to maintain this control and any challenge to what the ghost considers right. Righteousness is the main drive in this case. Any disagreement is met with considerable opposition. This is the boss who must always be right in the eyes of employees, or the parent who will not cede authority in the least.

從一開始就努力爭取偉大，不要接受比這更少的東西！

Cóng yī kāishǐ jiù nǔlì zhēngqǔ wěidà, bùyào jiēshòu bǐ zhè gèng shǎo de dōngxī!

19

DIFFICULTY AT THE BEGINNING

Your discontent begins with just one seed.

Failure begins with one small slip.

Do not let failure be an option.

Therefore, you must control from the beginning.

Strive only for greatness from the beginning and do not accept anything less than this!

THE UTMOST CONTROL. Once control is gained, it cannot be lost. This is anathema to this living ghost and amounts to invasion of one's self as far as living ghosts perceive it.

Preferably control should be gained from the very beginning so that there is no room for others to cause error. The ghost so disposed will also find little room to teach. This is beneath it and is therefore left to others of lesser ability. Here, the adages which govern are: "Those who can, do. Those who can't, teach," and "Failure is not an option." Perfection thus reigns, and is a standard applied to all.

There are immediate repercussions for this approach, however. This living ghost does not always share its standards with other beings, meaning that others may never actually be able to realize when they've missed the mark. They are left only to pick up the pieces while the ghost berates and, in some cases, bruises. Sometimes, the ego is not the only thing that gets bruised. Worse still for those around the living ghost who look to it for guidance. Again, it cares not to teach, but those in the lower station had better know. This living ghost is quite adept at helping to mold others into living ghosts.

只有理由才能保存一個人。拋開你的心，世界將
尊重你。

Zhǐyǒu lǐyóu cáinéng bǎocún yīgèrén. Pāo kāi nǐ de xīn, shìjiè jiāng zūnzhòng nǐ.

20

The intellect can dissect the 10,000 things, and dissection is understanding.

It allows one to keep wealth, but cannot stop evil.

Beautiful words will sell, and flattering conduct leads to control of others, for we are all creatures enslaved to feeling, and this is natural.

A high status is a natural rank to covet.

If a human is corrupted, toss them in the mud. This is clinging to Reason.

It is by reason alone that one can be saved. Set aside your Heart, and the world will honor you.

THE MIND IS TO BE CONTROLLED. The mind of the living ghost only recognizes ghosts. Its logic is one of separation, repetition, and self-reference. The mind allows one to think through, to realize. For the living ghosts, however, the mind becomes a room full of fun-house mirrors.

If one gives you words that are flattering, this is meant to evoke positive emotions. For a hungry ghost that embodies this virtue it is hollow comfort, if not foreboding and uncomfortable. Emotion is seen as a point of control, a tool that if used properly, can be used to control others. A sharpened mind often grants the opportunity to use the flattering words of others to its own advantage.

For the ghost that sits with this attribute and accepts its meaning, relationships with others become meaningless. The intellect sharpens, the heart dulls, dries, and shrivels to a small, hard pit. The ghost who embodies this virtue is unconcerned with matters of "good" and "evil," recognizing these are only part of the experience of the thinking mind.

For this living ghost, the mind is only a tool leveraged to accomplish goals or a blade used to separate concepts. As such, the mind must be kept very keen. That which dulls acuity is to be avoided at all costs. This is the space of intellectual elitism taken to a dizzying degree.

This approach, which also finds little value for "matters of the heart" can lead to a ghost who is coolly logical, preferring to remain in the shelter of tangible concepts and abstract proofs. It can also give rise to a ghost who possesses a predatory logic, justifying abuse or untoward behavior as being acceptable manifestations of abstraction. If moderated, the ghost can learn to be around others and to understand (although not always act upon) social cues. Taken to an extreme, this living ghost will find itself counted as a psychopath.

完整的心臟不能重新接受這個世界⋯從這裡，硬度⋯從硬度，沉重⋯從沉重，永恆。

Wánzhěng de xīnzàng bùnéng chóngxīn jiēshòu zhège shìjiè...Cóng zhèlǐ, yìngdù...Cóng yìngdù, chénzhòng...Cóng chénzhòng, yǒnghéng.

21

You have asserted your will.

You have left no thing alone in your drive to influence...

Let others scurry about, but only as far as you could control all eventualities.

Anxiety has been the calling card you've given to others, but in truth the anxiety is yours to have.

The full heart cannot take in anew the world as it is...from this, hardness...from hardness, heaviness...from heaviness, perpetuity.

THE NATURE OF THE GHOST IS TO ANCHOR ITSELF TO SOME-
THING OR SOMEONE. In this passage, we see a ghost that anchors
itself to the world purely through its own will. There is no logic,
there is no material fetter. There is no want to create. This ghost only
wishes to continue existing. Presence is the goal. In order to have
presence, other beings are required. This is true only insofar as they
are a means to establish one's own presence.

This ghost will control others but does not necessarily wish to
lead them. This is one who wishes to have the attention of all, but
this is counterbalanced by a presence which is unsettling to others.

This ghost will control the behavior of others by eliciting anxiety
within them, but will never recognize the anxiety that often sits at
the center of its own being. This ghost is not afraid of the idea of
death, but is mortified by the idea of its own nonexistence. As in the
previous passage, there is an illness in the heart.

The heart of the ghost hinted at in this passage is filled with an
anxiety or perhaps even a dread which it cannot fully artictulate.
There is only room for this anxiety because the heart is thoroughly
and totally full. As such, there is no room to accommodate the integration of new experiences nor is there room to grow in life. There
is only room enough to live, to exist—even if this proves hollow. The
goal for this ghost is to be the last living being in the universe because the anxiety, the dread raise by the prospect of "not being" is too
much to contemplate.

確保你在所有的榮耀中被看到！

Quèbǎo nǐ zài suǒyǒu de róngyào zhōng bèi kàn dào!

22

THE VIRTUE OF GRANDIOSITY

A great state shows the world that it is so. For then, all unite under its banner.

By extension, the quiet person conquers little, and being lowly makes one a victim of inertia.

If you act humbly, you will remain invisible and if you are flamboyant, it will force attention.

Make sure you are seen in all of your glory!

Unite people in deference to your magnanimity and stature, proving just how good you are!

IN THIS PASSAGE, WE FIND ANOTHER FORM OF GHOST THAT STANDS IN STARK CONTRAST TO THE ONE MENTIONED IN THE PREVIOUS PASSAGE. Whereas the previous ghost wished to be the only being in the universe, this ghost wishes to be recognized by every being in the universe. This living ghost thrives on accolades, awards, and the kind words of others.

There have been several types of ghosts that seek to capture the minds, attention, and even affection of others. In this case, the ghost does not wish to control with an iron fist. The ghost wishes to lead as the Pied Piper led his rodents. They came as willing participants, and ghosts showing this virtue want willing participants. It wants those who are willing to sit at its feet and swoon. Here, the ghost will use speech, extravagant gestures, and flattering words in order to control the minds of those around it by causing the blood to quicken and the breath to be stolen. They can be quite friendly, and even quite generous, laughing, joking, and complimenting to no end. That is, until someone tries to steal the spotlight...

Then, the face will darken, the blood will quicken, and the teeth will clinch.

緊緊抓住世界會產生鬼魂。

在眾人的犧牲下，眾神會變老，變胖。

最終，眾神將以鬼魂為食，從而成為鬼魂，這些將結合幽靈般的美德。

Jǐn jǐn zhuā zhù shìjiè huì chǎnshēng guǐhún.

Zài zhòngrén de xīshēng xià, zhòng shén huì biàn lǎo, biàn pàng.

Zuìzhōng, zhòng shén jiāng yǐ guǐhún wèi shí, cóng'ér chéngwéi guǐhún, zhèxiē jiāng jiéhé yōulíng bān dì měidé.

23

Conduct yourself in accordance with your own nature.

Clinging to the world gives rise to ghosts.

The gods will grow old and fat on the sacrifices of the people.

Eventually, the gods will feed on ghosts, thus becoming ghosts themselves, and these will combine the ghostly Virtues.

Thus, even holy men become ghosts,
Able to nourish neither body nor spirit.

Religiosity is no escape. Indeed, it is simply another divergent trail on the Path of the Living Ghost.

INERTIA IS NOTHING MORE THAN THE TENDENCY OF AN OBJECT TO MAINTAIN ITS STATE WITHIN WORLD, EITHER OF MOVEMENT OR OF STILLNESS, UNLESS ENERGY IS BROUGHT INTO THE SYSTEM, OR ENTROPY DISSIPATES THE ENERGY WITHIN THE SYSTEM. On earth, everything eventually stops moving due to this entropic process. This will happen unless more energy is introduced into the system. It must be acted upon by another force, or it will stop moving, growing, and evolving as living beings.

This premise works on a psychological plane as well. The psychic effects of life are just as subject to inertial effects as is a weighted pendulum. Popular psychology tells us that in many ways, we create the environment around us by our own actions. To some extent this is surely true. We have the ability to shape reality through a sequence of behavioral choices—for better or worse. When a person gets stuck, though, things get complicated, as they begin to lose a sense of control over the world. The living ghost, any ghost, is mired in its own thoughts to an extreme degree, and its actions will match this. As a consequence, the reality of a living ghost becomes a hostage to its own behavioral rut.

To say then that one has embraced inertia implies an even further step. The ghost is stuck in repeated patterns and may even acknowledge its state. However, in this case, the ghost begins to enjoy the process of wallowing in the space in which it exists with no eye toward change. It finds itself reveling in the valley in which it is mired. Stagnation becomes a statement, and the mud sucking at its feet becomes a friend. In many cases, this may be its only friend. Once one recognizes loneliness as an entity, one is rarely ever lonely. Likewise, once inertia becomes recognized as a way of being, change can become quite difficult, if not nearly impossible.

It should be borne in mind, that this aspect of the living ghost may be passed down from one generation to the next, as an elder generation teaches younger generations that they are incapable of doing the work of making any change. It can also be bred by having one always do for another. This is learned helplessness. Taken to an extreme, it can give rise to ghostly behavior insofar as it can impair one's skill in, or even the impulse toward, social interaction. The propensity toward ghostliness is further demonstrated in the ability of enabled helplessness to compromise physical upkeep, and lastly to the extent which it damages the spirit of the individual who is receiving the "help." This last outcome usually only comes after an extended period of time, and still requires recognition on the part of the living ghost. By this point, the issue may be moot.

畫地
為牢

從最早的時代開始灌輸灌輸了構造的美德，並確認⋯

Cóng zuìzǎo de shídài kāishǐ guànshū guànshūle gòuzào dì měidé, bìng quèrèn...

24

Nothing works like ceremony to unite people under heaven.

Ceremony is best undertaken from an early age, for this allows it to become indoctrination.

Indoctrination from the earliest age inculcates the virtue of conformation, and confirmation...

This will provide you with safe limits and acceptance of one's place within the grand scheme of the 10,000 things.

Let this conformity nourish you as a mother nurtures a child, yet with stale milk devoid of life force.

Thus, you will have the appearance of strength of deep roots holding fast.

In truth, the roots will weigh you down and your trunk will be rotten inside.

This is a hollow life, everlasting.

MANY GHOSTS WILL TAKE IT UPON THEMSELVES TO INDULGE IN CERTAIN TYPES OF TRADITIONS AND ACTIONS THAT HAVE NO SPECIFIC EFFECT UPON THE INDIVIDUAL GHOST.

In fact, these behaviors often affect those around it more than they affect the individual itself. The ghost who embodies this virtue is set upon those behaviors, not just for itself, but for others around it.

This amounts to control of behaviors generally passed from one member of a group to another. This transmission of behaviors may be minor, such as not eating certain kinds of food, or dressing in a certain fashion, or sleeping and waking at a certain time. This attempt to control a person's behavior may take on more drastic manifestations. A parent may tell a child that he or she is not allowed to play with certain other people, or that a certain religion is inherently evil. This type of behavior affects those around the locus of behavioral control, which can continue to ripple outward and across time to different generations.

The living ghost who embodies this attribute seeks to control behavior as a means to control individuals. These ghosts become attached to the ability to control behavior and to elicit certain desired responses from those same individuals. This type of ghost usually allows little room in its life for other people to get close, but it likewise will not let others around it have associations outside of the ghost.

The establishment of customs and culture within a small group sets in motion the selection of norms. Acceptable and unacceptable behaviors are established and certain behaviors are encouraged while others are discouraged.

A ghost who embodies this attribute does not easily tolerate differences in opinion about what is proper or improper, acceptable or unacceptable, and it will work to protect what it considers to be its own proper way. It considers confirmation of and concurrence with its own ideas to be the proper etiquette for strangers, and it is only through this agreement and validation that others are accepted at all.

This ghost values tradition, ceremony, and hierarchy. It is likely to show most strongly in individuals who exist in the law enforcement or military professions, as both of these require a certain amount of both discipline and indoctrination.

This indoctrination, in turn, becomes a form of sanctuary for the individual. The ghost no longer has to concern itself with individual thought and instead is given free rein to work within the confines of the larger group. In a certain way, the mind of this ghost is often not the mind of an individual, but is an individual component of a larger group mind.

This type of ghost can be very difficult to convince once its mind has been made up, as behaviors have been so deliberately conditioned and reinforced that the behaviors reach into the realm of blind obedience, or obstinance.

教化

不要輕易讓變化，因為這只會引發災難。

Bùyào qīngyì ràng biànhuà, yīnwèi zhè zhǐ huì yǐnfā zāinàn.

25

Truly, misery has no place upon happiness.

Try, absolutely, resolutely, to prevent catastrophe or unwanted experience.

Maintain your happiness and know that it can always be so.

Gird yourself against all possibilities, and take only those which would benefit you.

Do not let change come easily to you, for this will only invite catastrophe.

CHANGE IS A SOURCE OF MISTRUST. However, the living ghost who embodies this attribute has a broad mistrust of all things that do not stem directly from itself. This ghost believes that all things, once they become manifest, should in fact remain the same—now and forever.

This ghost considers resistance to change to be a source of positive influence on the world. As such, new ideas and the changes which they invariably bring are a source of fear and trepidation.

As in the previous passage, tradition is strongly valued, as is ritual and ceremony, as these are often the means by which tradition is upheld and transferred to others. Any variance from the norm produces either anxiety as the ghost tries to reestablish its normal routine, or anger as a ghost attempts to resist the change on its face, and this change may be the only factor in the anger felt by this ghost.

This ghost will find anxiety in most things, as it attempts to predict and control its environment and those within it. Clothing must be worn in a prescribed fashion and in a certain way, food must be prepared according to very strict guidelines, and social interaction should be both controlled and limited.

Innovation is unlikely, as this requires that the ghost think outside of the box. Technology is perplexing (if not overtly disturbing) to this ghost. Adaptation of any sort, in fact, can be sufficient to cause the heart to become even harder, and the mind more resolute as a reaction to change that it cannot place under its own influence.

This ghost is not only trapped in its own habitual behavior, but many times it is also trapped in a specific period of time. This ghost has great difficulty accepting the persistence of change through time.

把你的意志告訴全世界，但不要說出你不能放下
的東西。

Bǎ nǐ de yìzhì gàosù quán shìjiè, dàn bùyào shuō chū nǐ bùnéng fàngxià de dōngxī.

26

GOVERN YOUR MANNER

Maintain your habits and manner in the world in a strict fashion.

Restrict yourself and prohibit that which you cannot control.

Use the tools at your disposal to maintain this, through sharp word and through heavy, measured action.

Be cunning if necessary, and be violent if you must, especially within the realm of the mind. Others will fall into line, and so too should you.

There are times when ruthlessness becomes a virtue.

Assert your will upon the world, but do not call out that which you cannot put down.

ALL OF US LIVE IN A WORLD OF ILLUSIONS. We live in mirrored rooms that reflect a "self" image back upon ourselves a hundredfold. It is an image with cannot be avoided, for we know how we are—or at least we think we do.

The virtue found in this passage, however, speaks not to a living ghost's own self-delusion, at least not directly. Rather, this passage echoes out, referring to the illusion that the ghost shows to others. This passage is concerned with the control of a social image.

For this ghost, image is everything. Some ghosts will glimmer with otherworldly beauty, mesmerizing prey by dazzling it. Others will assert themselves through the sheer gravity of their presence even if this presence induces fear or shock in others. This ghost is concerned more with controlling its self-image then how that image is actually processed by those around it on an emotional level.

This living ghost is very capable of subterfuge, and its capacity for manipulating others around it through image control is only matched by its own capacity for self-deception. Generally, this ghost will place a high value on the physical appearance of both self and others. It has little recognition that the image others see is no more real than a mirage in a desert.

The trouble comes when the image begins to break down. Glamour gives way in the face of the most minute imperfections. This is both inevitable, for the body must fail, and for this ghost also untenable, as this image which others see is all that sustains it.

讓自己只參與你周圍可以看到的世界，但僅限於此！

Ràng zìjǐ zhǐ cānyù nǐ zhōuwéi kěyǐ kàn dào de shìjiè, dàn jǐn xiànyú cǐ!

27

DO NOT TOLERATE MYSTERY

Take only as truth those things which you can see and strongly encourage others to take this stance, even if this means strong argument is called for.

Do not let those around you blunt their own sharpness, for this reflects upon you, as well. It will dull your own acuity.

You are a human ghost alive in a human world.

Allow yourself to both love and hate as is necessary.

Ensconce yourself firmly in the realm of human experience.

Involve yourself only in the world you can see around you, but only that!

Mystery is a waste of time…

IN THIS PASSAGE, WE SEE NOT ONLY THE DENIAL OF MYSTERY AND THE UNSEEN, BUT ALSO INTOLERANCE THEREOF. The senses are trusted, but only insofar as can be quantified and corroborated by measurements and machines. This ghost will not only deny what it cannot see, touch, feel, taste, or smell but will become agitated at the suggestion that there may be something that it cannot experience directly.

The living ghosts embodying this virtue find the only meaningful thing to be the full experience of the body and the mind within the human realm. They are concerned with intensity of experience, but not necessarily with the content or context of that experience. The ghost is encouraged to seek out extremes in behavior and experience. For this ghost, there is no heaven or hell, no God, no devil, and no meaning beyond what the physical body grants.

Those who believe in unseen things will at the very least cause consternation for the living ghost, and at the most frustrated rage as it rails against what it considers to be stupid, insipid, and devoid of value. Instead it tries to weigh its time and experience through metrics which are "verifiable " and "true." More than this, the ghost uses these gauges to measure the time and experience of those around it, and will often base its treatment of other beings on how closely their beliefs and actions mirror the worldview of the ghost.

不要讓心臟成為你力量的源泉，因為你已經得到了一個身體…在別處尋找其他精神減少了這個的重要性…

Bùyào ràng xīnzàng chéngwéi nǐ lìliàng de yuánquán, yīnwèi nǐ yǐjīng dédàole yīgè shēntǐ…Zài biéchù xúnzhǎo qítā jīngshén jiǎnshǎole zhège de zhòngyào xìng…

28

If you are to possess virtue, do not act as a child would.

There is no innocence to be had in mystery. This is just laziness, and should not be tolerated.

Do not assume that you are safe from the slings and arrows of life merely because you possess "mystery."

Do not admire that which is venomous, but respect it. If necessary, use it.

If you are male, be a male.
If you are female, be a female.

Let only this be your harmony.

To do other than this is to lessen the meaning of both.

There is no increase to life other than what you can do during life. Do not wait for something afterward…this is a fool's bet…

Let not the heart be the source of your strength, for you have been given a body…Looking for some other spirit elsewhere lessens the importance of this…

TO LOOK AT THE MYSTERIOUS LEADS ONE TO THINK THAT THERE ARE SHADES OF GREY, THAT THERE ARE SUBTLE GRADATIONS IN THE WORLD. For this ghost, this is a lie, and is not tolerated. This passage encourages one to embrace one's own nature whatever that may be, for better or for worse. This is the only way to excel, and this is the only way that is acceptable.

In the same way, the living ghost that embodies this virtue will strive to recognize what it considers to be the "true" nature of things in the world, for better or for worse. In truth, this ghost only sees others as objects, falsehoods, and illusions. It is aware of the state of its perceptions and accepts them as being truths.

Lastly this living ghost has no tolerance for the guile, subterfuge, guise, or flowery words of others. It hears lies where there are none and plumbs the depths of inner motives in even the simplest of interactions in order to sniff out the tiniest hint of what it considers to be inauthentic.

This passage points not only to the desire to be "right" or "correct." Many of the passages encountered thus far have laid out this dynamic in fair detail vis-à-vis the living ghost. In this passage, however, there is also an element of self-righteousness which surfaces for this being. This ghost assumes insult before insult is given, and when none is given, will go looking for it. In this case, illusion is not just falsehood to be avoided, but an affront to the inherent dignity of the individual.

反對自己，衡量他人。

反對你的成就，衡量他人。

對你的家，衡量他人。

反對你的文化，衡量他人。

Fǎnduì zìjǐ, héngliáng tārén.

Fǎnduì nǐ de chéngjiù, héngliáng tārén.

Duì nǐ de jiā, héngliáng tārén.

Fǎnduì nǐ de wénhuà, héngliáng tārén.

29

THE CULTIVATION OF INSTITUTION

"What is well planted is not uprooted; what's well-preserved cannot be looted!"

Raise your children and your grandchildren in the ways that you have learned, let your habit be theirs.

Cultivate pattern in your home, and that you will be.

Cultivate it in those around you, and so shall you live long.

Cultivate it in the world, and so shall you be immortal...

Therefore:

Against yourself, measure others.

Against your accomplishments, measure others.

Against your home, measure others.

Against your culture, measure others.

Let Judgment be your guide.

This is a strong base, and not all things are equal.

THE CULTIVATION OF INSTITUTION IS THE CRYSTALLIZATION OF HABITS, PRACTICES, EVEN PROCLIVITIES WITHIN A GROUP, EITHER LARGE OR SMALL. The living ghost who thrives on this seeks to establish and instill into others aspects of rigidity and behaviors of dull repetition.

Institution is formed in order to groom behaviors, and with the right leadership, institution can affect large masses of individuals. This is mass production of living ghosts on a colossal scale. Dull-eyed masses repeating slogans, mantras, or prayers with slack-jawed, slurred precision.

This passage refers to one of the multitudes of grey individuals. Head down, waiting patiently for the message that will serve to reinforce its beliefs as a starving child waits for the first bite of food in several days.

The construct of institution yields a point of measurement against which other people are judged. The ghost showing this virtue will do just that. Indeed, that may be all that this ghost knows. This may be the creation of ideology at its most inchoate stages.

This ghost understands tradition and values it greatly, but the installation of institution requires nothing less than repeated action through time. Tradition is the behavior that brings one to specific point in time. Institution is that which governs the behavior of others over time. Sometimes, institution and tradition are the same. At other times they are vastly different.

沒有知識只會遺憾，因為一個人的時間，身體和
心靈都會花費。

Méiyǒu zhīshì zhǐ huì yíhàn, yīn wéi yīgèrén de shíjiān, shēntǐ hé xīnlíng dūhuì huāfèi.

30

Very few people regret having too much information, ignorance is to be feared.

The greatest Reason is elegant, and elegance must be experienced as part of its nature.

A mansion can only truly thrive on manicured land and with a rounded belly full of grain.

Failure to have these will result in nothing but regret as one's time, body, and mind become spent.

THIS PASSAGE RECOGNIZES THE VALUE OF LOOKING BACKWARD. This attribute is one that allows one to see through time, but only the past. Mired in nostalgia, this ghost sees only the past which we wish had become the present. The "gift" of hindsight is often nothing more than the curse of knowledge about what could have been.

The mind must be kept in check or it will run wild with suppositions. We ghosts know this, yet can do little to stop the momentum of deep regret once it begins. This is not a moral failing; it is merely the nature of a ghost.

This is true even when one considers that one has done nothing wrong in its pursuits. It can also be true when one wishes to have done more with its time. However, realization is not natural to the ghostly way of being. As such the living ghost is much more likely to spend time with regret about the stunted realization of its desires and goals over time. It has surrendered to obsessive rumination.

Regret becomes a refuge in which the living ghost can sit with itself, hands in its lap, shoulders hunched, with the mantra "I told you so..." ringing in its ears.

在世界上發現自己大膽而強大，你會發現自己與
地球聯繫在一起。

Zài shìjiè shàng fāxiàn zìjǐ dàdǎn ér qiángdà, nǐ huì fāxiàn zìjǐ yǔ dìqiú liánxì
zài yīqǐ.

31

HOLDING TO THE ORIGIN

The Earth is your domain, but the Earth also holds you.

It is a natural thing, as mother to child…

If you, in turn, close your eyes and still your action, you will lose that which anchors you. You will never recover.

If you are small upon the Earth, you will have little impact in the world.

If you are soft upon the Earth, you will have little impact in the world.

Find yourself bold and strong in the world, and you will find yourself attached to the Earth.

CLING TO THE EARTH! Chain yourself to its countenance. It is this whence you came, and you should endeavor always to stay here. Such is the logic of many a ghost, living or dead.

The Earth is the home of all beings we yet know of, and the goal of the living ghost which embodies this passage is to realize dominion over it and those which reside upon the Earth. This ghost seeks to leave an undeniable impact upon the Earth and control over that which it views as its kingdom.

The ultimate outcome of this stance is that the living ghost has tied itself to the Earth in such a way that it will continue to live on even after the body itself has ceased to function. This is nothing less than the transition from a living ghost to that of the ghost of the deceased. This is a fate that can befall both captains of industry and beggars alike. In the first case, the spirit of the living ghost is too strong to die, having been taken too soon in its own eyes. In the second case, it is sustained by regret and want.

作為一個幽靈，你已經放慢了速度，產生了慣性，這改變了所有…

你的想法發生了變化，你被這種慣性所塑造…

Zuòwéi yīgè yōulíng, nǐ yǐjīng fàng mànle sùdù, chǎnshēngle guànxìng, zhè gǎibiànle suǒyǒu...

Nǐ de xiǎngfǎ fāshēngle biànhuà, nǐ bèi zhè zhǒng guànxìng suǒ sùzào...

32

NURSING GHOSTLY VIRTUE

As a ghost you have slowed yourself, giving rise to inertia, and this changes all...

Your thinking is muddy and your Shen spirit is further shaped by inertia...

Yet many of you will still seek empty accolades to hang on your belt as you might wear a withered noose around your neck.

So, you trudge on...heels dragging.

THERE ARE THOSE OF US WHO CLING TO THE LAST VESTIGES, THE DYING EMBERS OF PREVIOUS ACCOMPLISHMENTS. We smile upon those things we accomplished with little regard for forging something new in our lives.

This ghost will always see some previous time as a Golden Age to be held close to the heart and revisited regularly. It worked hard for the accrual of accolades and commendations, but then it all stopped. It wants for more, but has no idea how to begin again, and lays no foundation for new achievements. Occasionally, this ghost will bring out its laurels from the mothballs, stale and too long gone to be recalled by others.

The eyes of this ghost see only earlier times filled with shimmering glory and adulation, and it therefore pays little heed to what is right in front of it. This is, perhaps, the happiest type of illusion, but it is also one of the hardest deceptions to recognize, and even harder to accept.

That being what it is, the living ghost will work to maintain this image even in the face of the unbearable march of time. Make no mistake, this is not about medals or trophies, handshakes or kind words. It is about the memory of who one was when these things took place. The ghost wants to remain there, as that person, forever.

If this former time is not recognized by others, this ghost often sinks into deeper depths, depression tinged with despondency. At other times, it may simply deride those around it for not having recognized the value of what it had accomplished. To an outsider, it will appear as a former life. Yet from the ghost's perspective, it will have every bit of common urgency as will of the immediate actions of the present day, if not more so.

我們都將死去，強度是別人唯一能看到的東西。

Wǒmen dōu jiàng sǐqù, qiángdù shì biérén wéiyī néng kàn dào de dōngxī.

33

THE OVERESTIMATION OF LIFE

"Abroad in life, home in death."

It is said that there are 13 avenues of life, and 13 avenues of death.

It is also said that the man who lives life with intensity will find his way onto the pathways of death.

The catch is that we are all going to die, intensity is the only thing that will be seen by others.

It is said that the good person can go abroad in life and not suffer misfortune...

But death is the very fruit of life, it is the outcome of a life lived...

IN EARLIER PASSAGES, THERE WERE SOME LIVING GHOSTS THAT WERE AFRAID OF DEATH, AND THERE WERE SOME THAT RECOGNIZED DEATH, BUT WHO LIVED IN ORDER TO AVOID IT. This passage is concerned with that living ghost who not only embraces death, but lives by seeking it out. This is a ghost who seeks out danger for its own sake without regard for its own well-being. This is not merely the frenetic pursuit of the adrenaline junkie, for they wish to continue living so as to find the next plateau. Here, the living ghost posits that there is little meaning to life and that pain cannot be avoided. The only feasible conclusion is a life unto death, and others should "live" accordingly.

In this case, it is considered that death is the only true key to life and to rebirth. Paradise for the living ghost embodying this virtue is ironically akin to socially sanctioned suicide. That is, as long as others are able to provide an audience.

Here, the key is a fundamental transgression. It is a deliberate crossing of boundaries. According to this ghost, the life one is given is a fleeting one, which must be lived in the most extreme manner possible. In this case, harmful acts may become routine as regard for safety and self-censor take a subordinate position to the focus on the destruction of one's personal "humanness" in lieu of more animalistic drives and action. There are very few of us, even as living ghosts, who embody this virtue, but there are some who find this as part of their way on the Path.

對於那些既不尊重你也不尊重你的人，在你眼前
把它們視為鬼魂。

Duìyú nàxiē jì bù zūnzhòng nǐ yě bù zūnzhòng nǐ de rén, zài nǐ yǎnqián bǎ tāmen
shì wéi guǐhún.

34

TRUST IN YOUR OWN ATTRIBUTES

Do not rely upon others to give you your heart.

Likewise, do not give your heart to others.

Treat with respect those who have given you respect and meet offense with offense.

To those who neither treated you with respect nor gave you offense, treat them as ghosts before your eyes.

MANY GHOSTS FIND THEMSELVES ALONE. This passage recognizes this state of affairs. This is mainly the case because we living ghosts are only fully allied to ourselves. It is a mistake, then, to allow others to affect the desires and actions of you, yourself, as a living ghost. In the same way, you should never fully volunteer yourself to be the subject of another person, as you should be free, and not a slave.

Recognize in others, dear ghost, the actions that have been taken on your own behalf. This being shows respect toward you in so doing. By the same token, recognize in others the actions that have been undertaken in opposition to your drives and your desires.

For the living ghost that embodies this behavior, or, more precisely this attribute, reciprocation is key. To this being, all relationships are merely quid pro quo. The ghost wants and will take. The ghost will give in return, but not equally. This is a means to conserve its own energy and to safeguard its resources.

Even enemies play a role for this ghost. Insult, offense, and hatred are all viable sources of energy for this type of living ghost. Think of the individual who thrives on negative feedback from others or who maintains certain unwanted behaviors solely for the reaction that they will receive from others. For this ghost, respect and infamy are key to its social relationships. All other traits are dead weight and will be shed very quickly.

讓你的話語投射你的力量，並讓你的力量重新出生。

Ràng nǐ de huàyǔ tóushè nǐ de lìliàng, bìng ràng nǐ de lìliàng chóngxīn chūshēng.

35

IN FORGETTING KNOWLEDGE

Forgotten knowledge is nothing but regret.

Strive to become learned in the world, and you will be involved in the world.

Let your words project your power, and always let your power be born afresh.

KNOWLEDGE THAT ONE DOES NOT RETAIN IS OF NO VALUE. If the information were of value, it would have been kept in mind. Slough off unneeded knowledge often. Shed obsolete knowledge as a snake would its old skin.

Many of us living ghosts live only in the past, reliving fond memories, and revisiting old regrets, but there are some who choose not to or who cannot remember the past. This ghost does not find value in the past except as far as it plays a role in the emergent present.

Here one's words come from the immediate present, without filter or consideration for consequence. This attribute is different than many of the ones that have come before it. Most of these attributes enable or cause the ghost to live predominantly in the past. In one case, the ghost chooses to be there. In another, the ghost is "pushed" in this direction by its own internal drive.

The point of importance here is the admonition not to regret that which is forgotten, as this is only sharpening the experience of the ghost as one hones a blade, by getting rid of excess material and pushing instead in a forward direction.

不要讓世界的幻覺帶給你。

只使用你曾經給過的新眼睛。

這些鬼眼會告訴你你需要的唯一真理。

Bùyào ràng shìjiè de huànjué dài gěi nǐ. Zhǐ shǐyòng nǐ céngjīng gěiguò de xīn yǎnjīng. Zhèxiē guǐ yǎn huì gàosù nǐ nǐ xūyào de wéiyī zhēnlǐ.

36

The further one goes, the more one learns...

The problem is that we never get to the place, the exact place, that we want to go.

Do not let the illusion of the world carry you.

Use only the new eyes that you've been given.

These Ghost Eyes will show you the only truth you will need.

SOME LIVING GHOSTS ARE REBORN WITH EYES THAT ONLY SEE EPHEMERAL PHANTASMS. The pupils, black and as big as saucers can see through time. For this ghost, the eyes can see some version of heaven. An impossible version of heaven, if any version of heaven is possible, and an even less likely version of the living world fills up the senses.

The ghost mind sees this movie reel as a deeper reality which only the individual living ghost can understand. In the mind of the ghost it is participating in heaven or hell presently. It need not wait for death to get to these far realms.

The most minute detail is displayed as if on a screen. Meanwhile, a faraway soundtrack wanders garbled into its ears, as if it were being heard underwater. The eyes can do nothing but stare, transfixed by the spectacle.

For this living ghost, there is a fundamental disconnect between what the ghost sees, hears, or touches and the objective reality around it. This ghost would rather choose to live in a world of its own making, which it perceives to be a secret reality, a deeper reality. In its mind there is a higher order in which it participates, either for better or for worse, and from which it can emerge only with great difficulty.

This ghost is very far along the path, and an outsider may never know what ineffable inner reality, whether ecstasy or damnation, the ghost may be facing.

通過陰雲密布的眼睛看到的最明亮的真理是慾望。

緊緊抓住真相，好像這是你唯一的營養。

Tōngguò yīnyún mìbù de yǎnjīng kàn dào de zuì míngliàng de zhēnlǐ shì yùwàng.

Jǐn jǐn zhuā zhù zhēnxiàng, hǎoxiàng zhè shì nǐ wéiyī de yíngyǎng.

37

THE FOLLY OF MODERATION OF DESIRE

The truth shown so brightly through your caul is that of Desire.

Yield to it...

Cling to it as though it were your only nourishment.

Indeed, for a ghost, it is thus...

Moderation in this is famine to the starving.

THE SPECTRAL IMAGE MENTIONED IN THE PREVIOUS PASSAGE IS NOTHING MORE THAN THE PROCESS OF DESIRE. Desire can be conscious, or it can be unconscious, but it is the supreme drive for any living ghost.

Desire can also be good or bad, but in all cases, there is a sacrifice to be made. Many living ghosts have the strong desire to protect family. Yet, as part of the process of fulfilling desire, they may get more defensive and more likely to anger, thus driving its family away from it. This in turn will have its own separate consequence, as the living ghost begins to feel alienated from the family it is trying to protect, and ultimately may lose even more of that which binds it to humanity.

The urge to protect does not stem from an act of pure love, but instead from the deep drive to control one's own environment. Intent matters.

This smothering desire is nourishment for many ghosts, it sustains them even when other relationships and experiences cannot do so. Why, then, would one want to curtail any desire, any drive which causes oneself to be? It is the raison d'être for any ghost and especially for the living ghost.

For a living ghost, it is necessary precisely because meaning, in the deeper sense, does not come easily to a many of us on this Path. This being what it is, meaning must come from somewhere, and moderation should never be applied to meaning. This is the logic of the ghost.

Remember though, that at its root, this logic comes from within the dried husk that is the living ghost, from the deep and often angry hunger in its belly…

靜止會變冷，習慣會讓人變成陰影⋯

Jìngzhǐ huì biàn lěng, xíguàn huì ràng rén biànchéng yīnyǐng...

38

GREATEST VIRTUE

Inertia is one of the greatest and most enduring attributes of the ghost.

Stillness breeds cold, and habit molds a person into a shadow...

INERTIA IS THE OUTCOME OF DESIRE. One is the drive and the other the manifestation. Cause and effect. Ghosts of the dead know of no other Way. The living ghost can choose it, and most will follow inertia to its utmost conclusion.

Stillness itself can be a blessing or a curse, and the further down the Path of the Ghost that one travels, the greater the ill-omen that stillness breeds. Like water left too long, this stillness can give rise to disease hidden deep within. This fetid spoilage begins, unseen as a darkening of the spirit. Given time, it will, indeed, it must show. It must surface. At this point, even stillness is driven. It is driven by forces that are very difficult to control.

以這樣一種生活方式生活。

Yǐ zhèyàng yīzhǒng shēnghuó fāngshì shēnghuó.

39

SETTING UP PRINCIPLES

The name defines the being, protect it.

Keep your fortune, but do not worry about what you have spent...

The only thing that you squander is life.

Live in such a way that you cleave to life.

TO SET UP PRINCIPLES MEANS TO FIND A CODE OF CONDUCT. If it is a principle, it can control one's behavior. The healthy individual feels that this code of conduct is a ruler against which practiced behavior is compared. In many cases, this is fine. For the living ghost however, principles quickly become rigid and uncompromising. As a consequence, behavior can easily become constricted or confined.

Under the right circumstances, principles can quickly become behavioral imperatives that can never be abandoned, even when they have outlived their usefulness. This failure to abandon what is no longer useful guides one even further down the path of the ghost. Not only this, but the unwavering adherence to principles quickly gives rise to righteousness. From righteousness emanate the seeds of judgment.

Adherence to principle also provides fertile ground for reputation to take hold. For the principled living ghost, this reputation and the honor which it commands are of paramount importance, even in the face of the suffering. When deeply held principles are upheld, there is often little consideration for the consequences visited upon others in the name of said principle. The principled ghost does not see this, as its eyes are clouded over with the "deeper meaning" of the principle itself.

In addition, there is little consideration as to the first origin of these ironclad principles. The ghost only knows that they ought to be adhered to, and that they are to be protected and revered.

努力分離，努力維護你的意志。

Nǔlì fēnlí, nǔlì wéihù nǐ de yìzhì.

40

Strive to separate, strive to assert your Will.

Do not leave yourself in quietude among the meek.

Use your voice, given so graciously, to separate yourself from the masses.

VERY OFTEN, THE LIVING GHOST IS AN EXPERT AT ASSERTING ITS OWN VIEWS. To the living ghost, Beings are separated into categories so that they are more easily controlled. The common division tends to be "us versus them." For the ghost, however, it is perhaps more appropriate to use the duality "Thou versus that" in relation to other beings.

In this case, the term "thou" is not viewed as an honorific, or as the transcendental principle. In the case of the living ghost, "thou" takes on elements of both reverence and of self-reference.

Embodiment of this virtue requires both separation and duality in order for the ghost to assert itself among the teeming multitudes in the world. More pointedly, it requires that the ghost hold itself to a different standard. Placing itself in a higher category, it abhors the mundane and creates a space where it becomes special. If there is a transcendental aspect to the way in which "thou" is used for the ghost it is only because the ghost has an internal imperative toward transcendence. Not transcendence of itself, but transcendence for itself, in its own eyes. Cognitive dissonance gives rise to this being. Compartmentalization is vital for its existence. Without it, there would be naught but chaos in the eyes of this living ghost.

培養優勢，並將它帶到墳墓和更遠的地方。

Péiyǎng yōushì, bìng jiāng tā dài dào fénmù hé gèng yuǎn dì dìfāng.

41

PERMUTATIONS OF REASON

You are only one among the 10,000 things in the material world.

You come from a mother and a father, and they too come from the same—this is the only unity that you will know.

The 10,000 things are sustained by Yin and contained by Yang, while the breath moderates both, and all under Heaven possess these.

The reasoning of the average person is vulgar.

What they find odious, unworthy, what they shun and make lonely, these should be your signets and talismans.

Cultivate superiority and take it with you to the grave and beyond.

THE TRANSCENDENCE ADMITTED IN THE PREVIOUS PASSAGE
GIVES RISE NATURALLY TO A SENSE OF SUPERIORITY. In this case,
no uninitiated being can ever hope to understand the material world,
the realm of the 10,000 things, as does this living ghost.

This ghost, given as it is to status and position in the world, cannot allow others to interfere through the deeper social interactions
that characterize close human relationships. Indeed, the "common"
person is held as being quite vulgar according to the self-referential
standards of this, the most royal of living ghosts.

If there is interaction between this living ghost and the standards
of the mundane, unwashed masses, it is only as an apophatic process,
as the ghost seeks to define itself by virtue of its being unlike these
common, lowly beings.

This can manifest in any walk of life, but perhaps the most troublesome of situations arises when a person claims to be accepting
of others, and yet still turns its nose up once they are with others of
similar status.

你可以向左走，你可以向右走，但總是前進。

永不退縮。

Nǐ kěyǐ xiàng zuǒ zǒu, nǐ kěyǐ xiàng yòu zǒu, dàn zǒng shì qiánjìn.

Yǒng bù tuìsuō.

42

SHAMELESS INDIFFERENCE

Do not be afraid to show little regard for what is "Right."

Rectitude is a fool's bet.

You can go left, and you can go right, but always move forward.

Never retreat.

If someone speaks to ridicule, let them speak, for it is a waste of their time. In truth, you have the last laugh.

This is because they are wasting the only finite resource that matters.

Always plodding and always plotting, this is your mantra.

INDIFFERENCE IS ONE OF THE MOST DISQUIETING AND LEAST HUMAN OF THE VIRTUES THAT A LIVING GHOST CAN EMBODY. In the previous passage, reference was made to a sense of superiority felt on the part of some ghosts based on status and position. There is still some regard for others as long as they are of the same status or higher.

When indifference is shown on a larger scale, this is even more insidious. In this passage, there is a profound indifference toward others more broadly. This ghost tends to be inhumane in its actions on and in the world. This ghost often exhibits ruthless behavior and has little regard for other beings around it. Other beings are recognized either as tools, as prey, or are of such little consequence that the physical death of this person would be a gift to the world.

This ghost would much rather allow others to expend resources before it even begins to mobilize and consume its own. This ghost will work to use the resources of others in order to advance its own goals and desires. In the eyes of this ghost, this is the only purpose for the existence of an entity.

如果你必須去，總是回來。 通過這種方式，您將
展示您難以理解的本質。

Rúguǒ nǐ bìxū qù, zǒng shì huílái. Tōngguò zhè zhǒng fāngshì, nín jiāng zhǎnshì nín nányǐ lǐjiě de běnzhí.

43

CONTINUAL RETURNING

Once you have found your home, root yourself there. Do not leave.

This does not have to be a place. It may be a thing, or it may be a person. It may even be an idea.

Attach there.

If you must go, always return. In this way, you will demonstrate your intractable essence.

BY ITS NATURE, THE LIVING GHOST CAN ONLY EXPLORE TO CER-
TAIN LIMITS. It can only stray so far. Its mind can only accept so
much before it must return to safe waters and known territories. All
ghosts exhibit attachment to some extent. Before the ghost finds this
subject of attachment it wanders searching for some meaning upon
which to hang its existence.

This passage speaks to the search for "meaning." This meaning,
however, does not empower the ghost. Once this connection with
meaning is formed, it serves as an anchor point from which it can
move, but from which it can never truly separate. As such, the ghost
can never truly progress past this point of repeated, refined, and reinforced focus. This object of focus becomes essential, even essence.

The ghost (even the living ghost) always lives in reference to it.
Tethered to this point of focus, at times even unwillingly, the ghost
must always return to it. This is both the strength and the weakness
of the ghost.

即使你活著，現在你已經被打破，彎曲，停滯，
腐爛，撕裂。

Jíshǐ nǐ huózhe, xiànzài nǐ yǐjīng bèi dǎpò, wānqū, tíngzhì, fǔlàn, sī liè.

44

THE ROOT OF EXISTENCE

You started life as a growing thing, vivacious, free, and pure.

No longer…

Now, you take a different form…

And even as you live, now you have been broken and bent, stagnant, rotten, and rent.

MOST OF US GHOSTS KNOW THE THINGS TO WHICH WE ARE AN-CHORED EVEN IF WE ARE NOT FULLY AWARE OF THE EXTENT TO WHICH WE ARE ENTANGLED. Existence for the ghost lies in this entanglement. As such, we cannot grow anew. The body may change over time, yet the ghostly state remains. The living ghost is not capable of living far beyond its fetters, its focus, its desires, its delusions, and hungers.

Listen, ghost! You have begun to move wholesale from one path to another. Here, the path diverges and the living human steps fully onto the path of death. No longer dragging feet, one on either path. Now a ghostly form in corpus.

According some lines of Chinese metaphysical thought, humans are granted 12 companions (spirits) who assist you to move through life. In the *Daodejing* it is said that those who follow the path of life (道養育生; *yang sheng dao*, lit. "nourishing life way") possess the 12 companions who allow the composite human to grow, change, and progress through life. The *Daodejing* also cautions that those who follow the path of death (培育死亡之道) also have 12 companions.

Living ghosts still have these 12 companions, although they are weakened parodies of themselves. In addition, the living ghost has a 13th companion: its own gnawing hunger. It sits in the pit of its belly pushing the living ghost to do that which would shorten its time. Hooks, whips, and blades, levied on the psyche of the individual, drive the living ghost to serve the dark needs of its Hunger, which leaves many of us barely human. In some cases, the living ghost intuits its nature, and is terrified. In other cases, they revel in this state.

有更深層次的驅動力，我們並不知情，而且我們無法控制。

美德只存在於我們自身這些深層領域的懷抱中。

這樣做，你就成了你的樣子。

Yǒu gēngshēncéngcì de qūdòng lì, wǒmen bìng bùzhī qíng, érqiě wǒmen wúfǎ kòngzhì.

Měidé zhǐ cúnzài yú wǒmen zìshēn zhèxiē shēn céng lǐngyù de huáibào zhōng.

Zhèyàng zuò, nǐ jiù chéngle nǐ de yàngzi.

45

Never lose sight of that which you embody.

But realize that you may not be in control of your body.

In most of us there are deeper drives to which we are not privy and over which we have no control.

Virtue exists only in the embrace of these chthonic domains of ourselves.

In doing so, you have become as you are.

THESE PREVIOUS VERSES ALL DETAIL THE PROPERTIES AND AT-
TRIBUTES OF THE TRUEST AND PUREST OF GHOSTS, AND MOST
OF US ARE JUST THAT TO SOME DEGREE OR OTHER, EVEN WHILE
WE LIVE. For many of us, life is just the process by which we learn to
become a living ghost. Is the process by which we assume a mantle
and receive the caul, which clouds our eyes. We do not start this way,
though. Sometimes the Path is chosen and other times, it is foisted
upon us. In either case, something steers us, unerringly, toward the
pursuit of our own inconsolable, gnawing void even as we are crowded and cramped among others on the same Path.

BOOK TWO

DÀO GUǏ

The Ghost's Progress

Live and let live, for we shall all return to some chaotic order.
At the root, no one is higher than another.
And you have turned your back on all except one...

鬼朝其飢餓的對象拉.

根据肠道的心灵！

Guǐ cháo qí jǐ'è de duìxiàng lā.

Gēnjù cháng dào de xīnlíng!

46

The Way of the Ghost points only in one direction.

The Ghost is pulled toward the object of its hunger.

And so, the Ghost does not fully command its own life.

Even the princes and kings among ghosts do not truly rule.

Ruled are they by those things of the world that feed the Hunger in the belly...

The Mind in accordance with the gut!

AS THE LIVING GHOST PROGRESSES FURTHER DOWN ITS INDI-
VIDUAL TRAIL ON THE PATH, IT VERY OFTEN BEGINS TO LOSE
ITSELF. It may still have a sense of "self," a seemingly unassailable
identity which it feels it can control, but very often, as time goes on,
autonomy is lost. At first, the ghost feels that it makes the decisions.
Over time, its darker drives, wants, and desires begin to take over the
decision-making process.

To say that the path of the ghost has one direction may seem
somewhat misleading, but once it is understood, it becomes almost
self-evident. The one direction is the direction determined by the
hungers and desires of the ghost. This is like a black hole from which
light cannot escape: all pathways will lead to the center of that mass.
Likewise, to the living ghost, all pathways will lead to the gnawing
hunger inside.

你已經達到了一個已經損壞的擴張點。 永遠向
前，永遠更好，永遠更大。

Nǐ yǐjīng dádàole yīgè yǐjīng sǔnhuài de kuòzhāng diǎn. Yǒngyuǎn xiàng qián,
yǒngyuǎn gèng hǎo, yǒngyuǎn gèng dà.

47

You have reached a point of expansion, which has caused damage. Always forward, always better, always bigger.

You are overburdened and bloated in the middle.

Hungering for self-satisfaction,

Gasping for self-righteousness,

When was the last time you contracted your Self?

FOR MANY LIVING GHOSTS, THE PUSH TO ASSERT ONESELF IS SO INTENSE THAT THEY DO NOT HAVE THE CAPACITY TO BACK DOWN, LET ALONE RETREAT. These ghosts cannot easily go within to view themselves. They are always focused on the outside, moving outward into reality. Self-reflection is done through a dirty and dulled mirror.

These ghosts are very good at manipulating others through speech and through action. These ghosts like to have others to follow them, and indeed, they gain energy from this. When asked to sit with themselves, these ghosts become very uncomfortable with the act of introspection. They are often afraid to look inside, to hear silence, or to look into the mirror.

These ghosts are very often unable to back down once they have made an assertion or have allied themselves with a cause. They often hold or have held positions of power, and they continue this trend. This is the boisterous boss, the drill sergeant, and the self-made entrepreneur.

For this ghost, other beings possess meaning only because they allow expansion to occur in the ego of the living ghost. If this ghost is confronted with a circumstance which forces it take a backseat or in which someone else has a strong personality, a conflict arises and the ghost will work to reinforce its own position, and at this point will have sought to pressure others to bend to their will.

在這，你看到自我價值。

有了這個，你就可以獲得自信。

以慈善的名義，搖動這麼多手，但從未接觸過一個人。

Zài zhè, nǐ kàn dào zìwǒ jiàzhí.

Yǒule zhège, nǐ jiù kěyǐ huòdé zìxìn.

Yǐ císhàn de míngyì, yáodòng zhème duō shǒu, dàn cóng wèi jiēchùguò yīgèrén.

48

ON BENEVOLENCE

When was the last time that you practiced benevolence without skill?

"Look what I've done!" you say.

Everyone knows what good you do, with the odious exception of those you would help.

In this, you see self-worth.

With this, you reach self-assurance.

In the name of Beneficence, shaking so many hands, yet never touching a person.

BENEVOLENCE, IF PERFORMED FOR THE RIGHT REASONS, CAN MAKE ONE MORE HUMAN. This is especially so if the benevolence practiced toward others raises them up so that they themselves become more fully capable of interacting with the world.

For the living ghost, benevolence takes a higher position in human interactions than the humans with whom the ghost is interacting. For the living ghost, the act of serving food at a soup kitchen is more important than the people who receive the food. This is commonly found in living ghosts who come from a particularly religious background. Which tradition is of little importance, as all religions and ideologies can give rise to this type of behavior.

The perversion of benevolence as it is shown here results in some ghosts using the guise of benevolence to rationalize other, often unrelated behaviors. This type of ethical subterfuge often has negative consequences for the individual and for those around it. For example, we may find a medical practitioner who takes medications from patients. The benevolence realized in this relationship is not the goal. It is a cover. At this point of the Path, the living ghost has assumed a mantle of inauthenticity, as the principle becomes the payout of behavior rather than its guide.

因此，偉大必須與小和我們分開。

Yīncǐ, wěidà bìxū yǔ xiǎo hé wǒmen fēnkāi.

49

JUDGING PERFECTION

In this Way that you walk, you have always had a higher Judge.

Not only God.

For some, there is none to be had but for what was given by one's ancestors.

You took all that was given there and began to divide...

This and that are the only viable means to see the world.

All else is ambiguity...

Therefore, the Great must needs be separated from the Small, and We from Them.

FOR SOME GHOSTS, JUDGMENT IS A REFLEX. Indeed, the ability to discriminate is often an adaptive exercise which leads to positive outcomes. In this case, judgment comes as a process of good or bad, and any situation must needs fit into either one of these two categories.

Often, this began when one was very young. A child learns by experimentation. But if the possibility of experimentation is cut off, the child does not get to know a spectrum of being. They view the world as a series of "either/or" propositions. Not only then does this ghost separate the world into black or white dualities, it also lets these dualities determine its behavior toward those two categories. Often, if one does not fit into the category considered positive by the ghost, it is treated badly, if not avoided altogether.

This is very common in ghosts whose early experiences were either truncated or impoverished. One is the curtailing of experience by another, while the second is the lack of exposure. Both represent neglect. This is often the process of ideologues who feel that one position is the correct position, and any other position is patently false. To be clear, the polar categorization inherent in religious or political systems themselves do not make ghosts. These ideas are meant to be used by individuals, and it is how these individuals react to this framework that determines how their ghostly nature will be realized.

鬼順鏡，作為反射顯示詛咒.

Guǐ shùn jìng, zuòwéi fǎnshè xiǎnshì zǔzhòu.

50

THE LUXURY OF DISCRIMINATION

With this, you can observe others, but never yourself.

Ghosts shun mirrors, as reflection shows damnation.

You have worked to conquer others, and little to rein in the Self.

AS A CONSEQUENCE OF PROFOUND RIGIDITY, ONE LEARNS TO DIS-CRIMINATE ONE GROUP FROM ANOTHER VERY QUICKLY. The living ghost at this point will very quickly begin to elucidate either the merits or the flaws of one category or another, but they do not often use the same keen vision on themselves. This is the realm of critics and commentators whose work entails the observation and ascription of value to aspects of physiology, psychology, or even culture.

Remember though, that here, the living ghost cannot look at itself in the same manner by which it judges others. There is a horror that comes from self-recognition for many ghosts, as they are able to recognize imperfection within themselves. However, this ghost exists in a space where it does not wish to be seen for the flaws it holds, either in Mind or in body. This simple act of observation becomes a house of mirrors from which it cannot escape.

聖潔是孤獨。

Shèngjié shì gūdú.

51

THE VIRTUE OF HOLINESS

You have worked to control, contain or explain all things.

Seldom have you participated fully in life, neither theirs, nor yours…

In this case, Holiness is loneliness.

IT IS LONG BEEN OBSERVED THAT MANY CHURCHGOERS ARE NOT TRULY HOLY. Holiness is a state that, depending on one's tradition, requires that there be some profane aspect against which to rail.

For the living ghost, holiness is twisted into the set of social constraints that may begin as a sincere wish to live a sacred life. When this social component takes precedence over the enactment of the sacred, the ghost can be found there. In this sense, it is a holy ghost. It is a holy ghost insofar as it clings to this holiness and righteousness as the only defining characteristics of its existence.

This is not to say that holy objects, relics, and symbols are of no value. Trouble is encountered when the ghost can only reach what it considers to be a holy state through proper application of these things. It needs the trappings of religion in order to experience the sacred. Ritual and artifice override energy and ecstasy.

This is the realm of officiants of mega-churches and very rich cults. These ghosts to not work for the betterment of the world as a whole. There is only consideration for the value that the flock holds.

你最近有人砍人嗎？血可能不在您的手上，但它
確實從嘴裡發出。

Nǐ zuìjìn yǒurén kǎn rén ma?

Xuè kěnéng bùzài nín de shǒu shàng, dàn tā quèshí cóng zuǐ lǐ fāchū.

52

ON VIOLENCE FOR ITS OWN SAKE

Have you cut anyone, lately? Blood may not be on your hands, but it can issue from the mouth.

The Ghost knows not silence, words always vomited out, shredding those who attend lower stations.

In this way, it conquers others.

THERE IS AN IMPORTANT QUESTION WHICH THE READER SHOULD ASK ITSELF: "HAVE YOU CUT ANYONE LATELY?" To cut in this context may not mean to cause physical harm, but to cut to the quick, nonetheless. Angry words may cause even deeper wounds. Many of us speak with barbed tongues, Poisoned words issue forth with ease. A single stare, icy cold, can reduce an adult to a child.

This ghost knows the effect that it has on others and has little concern for the effects of its violence. In many cases, physical violence can be defended against. One can fight back. With words of venom and decisive razor-like actions, there can be little if any chance to mount a timely defense against this living ghost. The vulnerable and weak are its preferred prey, and this ghost is a predator, whose ability to weaponize words becomes its hallmark.

To be at this place on the Path of the Living Ghost, there must be an exemplary command of language, both verbal and nonverbal. This ghost learned from an early age that its words are its Ways and Means in the world, and that verbal manipulation can be even more effective than overt physical violence. Sometimes not physically robust, but always very sharp of mind and tongue, this being will find within its would-be victims the fodder which it seeks. Likewise, the glib, silver tongue which represents this ghost can very quickly turn poisonous, especially if a person does not respond to its overtures. The rage which this causes will play out as barbed lashes from the vocal cords rather than blows from a fist—again a skill which was bestowed at an early age and learned through direct and often painful experience.

說說暴力是最真實的危險！

Shuō shuō bàolì shì zuì zhēnshí de wéixiǎn!

53

PROPER USE OF VIOLENCE

For you, an act of violence, either in deed or word, keeps you safe…

Safe from the ever-present threat of examination and reflection…

Even with softness there can be violence, as when parent manipulates child…

"Because I say so."

Spoken violence is the truest danger!

THREATS OF VIOLENCE KEEP OTHERS IN LINE SO THAT THEY DO NOT ASK QUESTIONS, SO THAT THEY DO NOT DISOBEY. This ghost knows that it knows best, not just for itself, but for others as well. Any challenge to this viewpoint is seen as weakening the ghost's power.

This condition is pervasive in the modern world, and at some point in the past, it may have been something of a useful standpoint. Now, however, this approach only serves to transmit illness.

This is a matter of violence upon violence upon violence. The offense comes not in the commission of violence but in the questioning of the violence itself. That violence is frequently used to reinforce other cultural aspects such as social standing, filial piety, gender expectations, and other parts of the human experience.

For many ghosts, the type of violence mentioned in the previous passage is constructive. It keeps others in line, and teaches the young to obey the elder. What this violence does, in reality, is to pass the status of living ghost from one generation to the next.

The previous passage speaks of a form of verbal manipulation that is much more subtle. This passage speaks to the shouted word as the medium par excellence for the conveyance of violence both between persons and between generations.

This state of affairs is very likely to give rise to successive generations of living ghosts. It is yet another way that the ghostly nature is transmitted down familial and community lines. In this case, the younger generations learn that they must fend for themselves both in word and in deed—a whole generation of wounded beings existing one or two steps from ferity.

隨著目的，方向和力量而移動。

不要試圖讓別人引導你，因為這是你的生命！

Suízhe mùdì, fāngxiàng hé lìliàng ér yídòng.

Bùyào shìtú ràng biérén yǐndǎo nǐ, yīnwèi zhè shì nǐ de shēngmìng!

54

ON ASSERTION

You have worked to mold, to shape…

Do not let it go.

This is your work.

Nothing is naturally perfect.

Everything requires refinement.

Continue in this way…

Move with purpose, direction, and strength.

Do not seek to let others lead you, for it is your Life!

WE GHOSTS ALL MOVE IN DIFFERENT WAYS. Some trudge slowly, others rage. All of us seek control—to impose our will upon the world and upon those in it. If the ghost has gotten just a small taste, a minuscule bit of control, it often will never relinquish its hold.

It is a falsehood to say that we living ghosts all walked onto the Path knowingly and with complete agency. This is much too simple. Most of us had a precursory circumstance which bestowed upon us the primary vestments of ghosthood. Mothers, fathers, friends, teachers, enemies. Any of these persons in our lives could have triggered an event that leads to ghostliness. Bullies, rapists, murderers might also contribute to this same process, taking away some semblance of humanity or at least subverting it for extended periods.

Once the living ghost begins to lose control over its environment, humanity begins to slip away even further. The ghost will then seek to assert itself within the world. Its sense of control and order is necessary to conserve and retain those human aspects that it still possesses.

The ghost's act of assertion can mean different things at different times on the Path. As with so many things, this move toward assertion exists on a spectrum across which the ghost may move as it continues its existence. At early stages, assertion is an act of stabilization. The ghost is young at this point and may be seeking to regain its humanity. It may crave humaneness and may be working to regain this aspect of its previous existence.

Very often, as the ghost continues its existence, the move toward humane behavior begins to slow. Spiritual inertia sets in. If left unchecked, it will even reverse course. During this time, the ghost begins to act with increasingly authoritarian tendencies. It begins to move in the direction of strict polarities and distinct categorization, and it begins to act on this.

Even further down the Path, the ghost begins to act in such a way so as to actively control others. Resistance will be met with anger, insult, or even physical violence. Thus, a new generation of ghost is born.

224

人們會尋求兩者兼而有之。

不要放縱這個。

劃分！

劃分！

Rénmen huì xúnqiú liǎng zhě jiān ér yǒu zhī.

Bùyào fàngzòng zhège.

Huàfēn!

Huàfēn!

55

INDULGING IN COMPLEXITY

Let one side be one side and the other be the other.

Let male be male, and female be female; the two natures are not the same...

The active leads, the passive follows, this is natural. Do not confuse the two.

People will seek to have some of both.

Do not tolerate this.

Divide!

Divide!

Show others by your example.

IN THE PREVIOUS PASSAGE, THERE IS MENTION OF POLARITY. Strict "either/or" classification would give one an allowance of, but only one, of two choices. One of which is "right" the other of which is "wrong."

How then do we arrive at this recognition of complexity when we are addressing what would appear to be an either/or decision? This would seem counterintuitive for most.

Here, complexity arises when one caters to the need to put everything into one of two categories. More importantly, these two categories must not fundamentally interact.

Complexity arises when the ghost feels the need to place other entities into these convenient categories so that it can more easily act upon those entities, either through control of these entities, or isolation from these entities.

Sometimes this living ghost uses this need for division to establish the usefulness of one being versus another as a pawn to be used, two possibilities to be pitted against one another. At other times, the drive to divide stems from the deep desire to maintain separation from what it considers to be a lesser group—the need for separation exists in order to assure purity.

你已經磨練了你的技能，達到了無人能爭議的程度。

保持這一點，讓它指導你的方式。

Nǐ yǐjīng mó liànle nǐ de jìnéng, dá dào liǎo wúrén néng zhēngyì de chéngdù.

Bǎochí zhè yīdiǎn, ràng tā zhǐdǎo nǐ de fāngshì.

56

THE PROPER USE OF SKILL

Skill is a point of demarcation…

Those who have it, know it, and those who do not, don't know it.

You have honed your skill to a degree that no one can dispute.

Hold this high and let this guide you on your way.

SKILL IS THE ACQUISITION OF KNOWLEDGE THROUGH REPEATED USE. Skills can come to any who are able to practice. This allows all individuals to add to the body of experience or knowledge involved in that particular skill.

When a ghost uses a skill however, there is often an element of exclusion. It is said by some that a master should never teach the student all that he or she knows. This is close to the thought process of the living ghost. For the living ghost, skill is meant to be held over others, dangled as if on a stick and unattainable.

Even this process can result in the realization of specific goals when one is teaching a student. One may want to illustrate one's skills in great detail so as to show the student what is possible. A teacher may tell the student that he or she may never attain this level in order to test his or her fortitude or to push the student further. This can help them break through barriers which stand in his or her way.

The ghost does not teach this way. This approach requires concern for the learning process of the student. The living ghost clings to its own knowledge for its own sake. It may even seek to learn new material, but this is not done for the betterment of those around the ghost. It is only done to add to the altar of excellence which anchors the ghost. Its skillset so refined that its existence is bound up by the one thing which has been so heavily emphasized for so much of its life. This is the athlete whose life revolves around the minutia of his or her sport to the exclusion of all else, or the model maker who must have all things "just so."

了解自己的自我重要性，讓別人被你的言行所吸引。

Liǎojiě zìjǐ de zìwǒ zhòngyào xìng, ràng biérén bèi nǐ de yánxíng suǒ xīyǐn.

57

THE VIRTUE OF GRAVITAS

Small things are anchored by the great, and you have let this guide you.

You live with "greatness" and this is a heavy weight to bear.

Know your own self-importance and let others be drawn to your words and deeds.

This, in turn, will anchor them with you...

MANY OF US HAVE A VERY REFINED SENSE OF OUR OWN EGOS, AND OUR OWN IMPORTANCE IN THE WORLD. We view ourselves as temporarily embarrassed millionaires simply waiting for the time when our hard work and resilience will reward us with our just desserts.

Fame and fortune are things to be worked toward, but the real fruit to be born of these is the impact that one has upon the world. In one's own eyes, one lies at the center of the world.

So it is for many ghosts. Wear bracelets upon the wrists and heavy necklaces around the neck, or handcuffs and shackles around the same. These are the trappings for something deeper—the hunger for recognition, or, more correctly the avoidance of the existential threat of invisibility to the world.

The recognition given to one by others, the adulation of one's followers, this all illustrates the gravity, the power, of one's own existence. And it is the blessing of one's own existence which one gives to the world. This is the way of the living ghost.

神秘！

如果你是真正的教師，你已經停止了這一點。

其性質之謎，無法觀察到。

試試看是浪費…

Shénmì!

Rúguǒ nǐ shì zhēnzhèng de jiàoshī, nǐ yǐjīng tíngzhǐle zhè yīdiǎn.

Qí xìngzhì zhī mí, wúfǎ guānchá dào.

Shì shìkàn shì làngfèi...

58

IMAGING THE MYSTERIOUS

Mystery!

You have ceased this, if you are of any true faculty.

Mystery by its nature, cannot be observed.

It is a waste to try...

There is no Being to be had.

No heaven, no hell.

Salvation stands only so far as one clearly sees what is

There is no deeper meaning in word or in name.

This is your mind and your way—exchanging sly, knowing smiles with Oblivion...

And it terrifies you.

MANY OF US GHOSTS LIVE ON THE EDGE OF A PRECIPICE. Some will look down into the nameless place. Most will turn their backs in order to avoid becoming part of the unknown.

The ability to name a thing allows one to begin controlling it. That which is mysterious only stands as such when it cannot be fully observed. Living ghosts are keen observers of their own domains and prefer things to be controllable, and thus nameable.

There is only one chasm, one space that fits this moniker of the mysterious for the living ghost. This is the hunger, the ceaseless, knowing space which we ghosts seek to fill. It lies in the belly, and while it has no teeth of its own, it will cause the gnashing of our own. It is fully capable of chewing us up slowly, and consuming what humanity we have left.

This is the only role that the mysterious plays for the living ghost. It is generally not embraced by many of us precisely because we do not have control over it. Make no mistake about this. Unfortunately, we living ghosts do not have as much control over the mysteries of life as we think we do. If we did, we would not be ghosts. This is the fundamental paradox of this passage. To be a ghost, even a living one, is a mysterious thing!

你擁有的起重機的頸部不能讓任何一個通過。

沒有營養，沒有知識！

Nǐ yǒngyǒu de qǐzhòngjī de jǐng bù bùnéng ràng rènhé yīgè tōngguò.

Méiyǒu yíngyǎng, méiyǒu zhīshì!

59

DRIVEN TO INDULGENCE

You have taken much in—your brain crammed full of flashing grey images—

"Sustenance" stuffed into your gullet.

The crane's neck that you possess cannot let any of this pass through.

No nourishment, no knowledge!

Left instead with an insatiable need to numb.

INDULGENCE IS A MEANS TO DISTRACTION. Whatever paths we have found in our lives have taken us to this place. We become oversaturated with the trappings of a hypermodern life.

Daily we work with "tools" which continually co-opt our attention and our intention. Social media becomes, after a point, less and less social, which is fine for a living ghost. Most of us prefer that, if we would care to admit it.

The devices we use provide us with the illusion of instant gratification, or at least access to it. In truth, however, we do not possess them. They possess us.

Those of us who are far along the path of the living ghost will notice that it becomes harder and harder for us to interact with others. Remember, this unwillingness to interact with others is one of the major calling cards of the living ghost. If we cared to call upon anyone.

Interaction with others is a form of nourishment, if it is done for the sake of beneficence and equanimity. If this means of nourishment is neglected, other conditions must be sought in order to fill the void, to numb the need within. Food, sex, drugs, extreme activity. Any and all of these are enlisted by the ghost in the cause of calming the encroaching unease felt deep within. Yet, like empty calories, these things will often leave one malnourished and with a greater hunger. The need is left unmet, the need arises again, and the cycle continues. It is an addiction to emptiness, and not an imminent emptiness, pregnant, and full of potential. Rather, the living ghost becomes attached to a desolate emptiness, a barren emptiness, a dry emptiness which does not allow roots to take hold nor for possibilities to spring forward.

你坐在折磨的沉默中，沒有人能看到你為了別人的利益而忍受的痛苦！

你被召喚殉難，你已經聽從了呼喚。

Nǐ zuò zài zhémó de chénmò zhōng, méiyǒu rén néng kàn dào nǐ wèile biérén de lìyì ér rěnshòu de tòngkǔ!

Nǐ bèi zhàohuàn xùnnàn, nǐ yǐjīng tīngcónglе hūhuàn

60

EMPTINESS AND NON-EXISTENCE

You have sat in tortured silence, no one can see the pain which you have endured for the benefit of others!

You are called to martyrdom and you have heeded the call.

Now, you contemplate your own existence, and find it wanting. Your mind tells you things you do not want to hear.

Some of the thoughts are yours, while others come from another space, another voice...

You have taken up Association with others who are like you to share your "longing" for emptiness.

You wear your bad luck as a badge of honor around your neck.

Having no faith, neither will others have faith in you.

Fellow ghosts on the Path, to be sure.

SOME GHOSTS HAVE A FOCUS, A SITUATION, AN ACTIVITY, EVEN AN ITEM WHICH PROVIDES THEM WITH JUST ENOUGH OF A FOCAL POINT THAT OTHER DARKER ASPECTS OF THE HUMAN CONDITION CANNOT TAKE HOLD. Hope is powerful medicine, and can help one regain one's humaneness.

Many living ghosts have lost this.

There are some ghosts who believe in only themselves. They have no means or desire to rely on others and, for them, this is fine. Their sole focus is their own existence. This is often the way of hedonists and solipsists.

This passage, however, speaks to the ghost who has faith neither in external world of things nor in itself or its own transformative inner experience. Often, this ghost has expended a great amount of energy in the process of "hope." And has been rejected by it many times. This ghost has been left wanting by those around it, at least in its own eyes. In most cases, this embittered state likely commenced at a very young age with an insult so grave that hope, one of the pinnacles of the human psychological experience, is stolen. Or worse, spoiled.

Remember, ghost: when hope is not available as a medicine, compassion may be the only thing left. Give this as best as can be done, and accept it as well as you are able.

你已經給了一個有罪和羞恥的舒適的家。 這是你的心臟，像一個老桃坑一樣乾燥和收縮。

Nǐ yǐjīng gěile yīgè yǒuzuì hé xiūchǐ de shūshì de jiā. Zhè shì nǐ de xīnzàng, xiàng yīgè lǎo táo kēng yīyàng gānzào hé shōusuō.

61

HUMILIATION'S INCREASE

You now show your own crooked path.

Others trod beneath you.

You have given guilt and shame a cozy home. This is your heart, dried and shrunken like an old peach pit.

Tired and wearisome, to both yourself and to others,

Herein, you dwell...

THERE IS A FAIR BIT OF DIFFERENCE BETWEEN SHAME AND GUILT. The ghost makes little distinction between the two. Shame is placed upon one by others. Guilt is that which one feels for one's own action or inaction.

This ghost sits in a place of futility, on a throne of repeated failure. "Why try?" becomes its mantra.

The ghost that does not try often suffers backhanded slights at the well-meaning lips of loved ones, or downright degradation. Shame begets guilt; they are not the same! This causes the heart to contract, and the orifices of the mind will close off. The spirit cannot move forth in order to interact with the world. So it stays and begins to fester. In some cases, this becomes spite felt toward others, but only at the beginning. Further along, this can easily become spite felt toward oneself. In both cases, it is an overburdened heart. World-weary, yes, but mostly sick of itself. Here, weakness will be found in the chest and disease will lodge there. Grief comes in waves as one experiences in slow painful detail a life left unlived.

這是地獄之門！

Zhè shì dìyù zhī mén!

62

THE PERIL OF A FULL HEART

Transcendent beauties held within the eyes,

Beauteous tones alighted upon the ears.

Freshness...

Saiety...

Contentment...

All of these elude, all because no room can be made in the Hearts of Ghosts.

This is Hell's gate!

All are encouraged to enter, yet none leave.

So, too, the heart,

Too full to contain and never being emptied of its burden,

Enlarged but weakened, sunken chest ever-expanding

To the crackling strain of spiny, brittle ribs.

ACCORDING TO CHINESE THOUGHT, THE HEALTHY HUMAN BE-ING SHOULD NEVER HAVE A "FULL HEART." The heart and mind are considered one. When the heart is full, the mind is full. When the mind is full, very little gets done.

For many living ghosts, the heart is the storage place of all that is gone wrong. The sum of the insults we endure, all of the abuse, and the accumulated weight of want or unmet need are stored there. This prolonged storage of unprocessed energy hinders change.

Change occurs when new, novel situations take place and are recognized as such. New relationships occur because one spirit (Shen) is able to meet other spirit (Shen). This is not considered a supernatural occurrence in Chinese thought. This Shen is merely the heart/mind's ability to project awareness into the external world.

In this line of thought, the heart is the conceptual, if not entirely corporeal space where the Shen is rooted. Shen, in turn, comes and goes as necessary. A full heart prevents this movement. If the heart is overburdened with this unprocessed energy, the heart becomes malnourished. Its ability to accept new experience is curtailed. Such social interactions of the type controlled by the heart will begin to suffer, and the ghost will sink deeper into itself, with despair increasingly becoming its most constant companion.

在你的州里孤獨，在你的存在中空虛，不願意接
受別人…

巨大的寂寞和灰色，沉重的空氣籠罩著裹屍布

即使如此，你仍然在教誨！

Zài nǐ de zhōu lǐ gūdú, zài nǐ de cúnzài zhōng kōngxū, bù yuànyì jiēshòu biérén......

Jùdà de jìmò hé huīsè, chénzhòng de kōngqì lóngzhàozhe guǒ shī bù jíshǐ rúcǐ, nǐ réngrán zài jiàohuì!

63

DIFFERENTIATION FROM VULGARITY

You have kept to your bookishness and shun vulgarity as you are high and mighty.

You laugh to hear laughter, without knowing genuine happiness.

Rushing headlong into the levity of the gods with no sense of the holy because you despise the vulgarity of the mundane.

Forlorn in your state, empty in your being, and unwilling to accept others...

Vast loneliness and sullen, heavy air hang as a shroud.

And even still, you pontificate!

SOMEWHAT IN CONTRAST TO THE PREVIOUS PASSAGE, SOME GHOSTS HOLD THEMSELVES IN VERY HIGH REGARD. They have much "faith" in themselves, and sometimes even a Higher Power. This is not ghostly behavior.

This living ghost lives according to ideologies and despises those who do not believe the same way, or perhaps even worse, pities them. This passage indicates a place on the path of the ghost where one chooses to shut others out, or even shun them.

All the while, they are incapable of fully participating in the ideology forming the bulwark of their own beliefs. This is the ghost that subscribes to ideologies and yet finds no fulfillment from them. Rites and rituals are practiced with emptiness of purpose and with exquisite, if useless precision. Thus, fulfillment is never forthcoming. Thus the ghost's behavior goes against their "sacred" ideology even as they speak loudly in favor of it.

你一直保持著自己的聖潔，並且獨自採取謹慎行事⋯

這是道！

Nǐ yīzhí bǎochízhe zìjǐ de shèngjié, bìngqiě dúzì cǎiqǔ jǐnshèn xíngshì...Zhè shì dào!

64

You have kept to your saintliness, and acted upon your own prudence alone...

This is the Way!

Shown benevolence radiates as light from the Sun.

In so doing, people remain at the foot of the Father.

This is the Way.

Striving for preservation, to keep thieves at bay.

This is the Way.

These are the ways of culture at large.

THIS PASSAGE SPEAKS TO THE ROLE OF INDOCTRINATION AND HIERARCHY WITHIN THE PATH OF THE GHOST. Many ghosts were raised into their state, or at least predisposed to it by the encouraging behavior (and in some cases the prodding) of others.

Many living ghosts find it necessary to buy into the belief system or systems to the exclusion of others. Sometimes, this is but an internal rejection of other thought patterns and belief systems. In other cases, the resistance may be violent at physiological or psychological levels.

Belief, in itself, is not negative as such. It is the behaviors enacted in the name of one's beliefs which are often the cause of so much pain in the world.

This passage speaks of the living ghost who moves as a zealot in the world. Belief systems become ingrained and can crystallize over time, much like scar tissue. Thus the scars of belief can keep us from exploring new options. Failure to recognize this process can be quite insidious, as it is often very subtle.

因此，你也開啟了禮儀。

這是虛偽的。

Yīncǐ, nǐ yě kāiqǐle lǐyí.

Zhè shì xūwèi de.

65

RECTITUDE OF VULGARITY AND SHUNNING PROPRIETY

You have expended vast stores attempting to quell vulgarity, but with no eye toward yourself.

Thus, you have also turned on propriety itself.

This is hypocrisy.

It is when people do not act of their own accord that piety and devotion become institutionalized.

Loyalty and allegiance are no longer human traits, but instead become issues of political import and social expedience.

This is the political sport of the living ghost.

THERE ARE SOME GHOSTS FOR WHOM A BELIEF SYSTEM PROVIDES JUSTIFICATION OF ONE'S BEING. This justification allows for behavior against both self and others which would otherwise be both unwanted and unwarranted. Violent behavior becomes the norm, and the raised voice is the only acceptable volume for the more powerful. Conversely, silence is the only acceptable stance for those held under the thumb.

In many cases, this may be seen in larger institutions, such as religious or social organizations. Often, however, this is learned within the familial setting. Children learn most quickly that which is the most apparently violent and "powerful." So it is passed on across and along generations. This is a transmission of energy—an inherited burden. This transmission of burden can be very difficult to break once it has been ignominiously bestowed upon an individual.

It is here that the individual learns loyalty, at the behest of a closed fist, and it is here that he or she must return to find the respect that they crave. This is not recognition in any grand sense, and may only affect an immediate group, such as one's family. It is, however, an attempt to cover the weakness which is still painfully felt, and which still brings feelings of failure.

蒼白，幾乎半透明，你展示自己。

Cāngbái, jīhū bàn tòumíng, nǐ zhǎnshì zìjǐ.

66

OSTENTATIOUSNESS IN HABITS

You choose to show:
your ideas, opinions, impressions, even the body...

Pale, nearly translucent, you show yourself off.

Your accomplishments and merits presented for all to hear...

Until the next thing comes along.

MANY GHOSTS SEEK THE SPOTLIGHT. Performers, players, and projection from the pulpit. Here is an image that is broadcast out to the audience, and one that the ghost is all too happy to oblige. Dramatic flourishes and eloquent words provide fertile soil from which adoration grows. To the audience, any multitude of wants and needs are enacted. To each spectator, this ghost stands as a mirror that only reflects them. One self and one other, each enthralled, enamored with what the other provides.

Each and every chance for some kind of immortality is embraced. In the mind of the ghost, whatever the present "audience," it knows that the throng exists only because there is a show to see. The living ghost is both the ringleader of the spectacle and the diversion itself.

For the ghost, though, the equation is reversed. You see, on the path, the ghost desires this spectacle even more than the audience does. The ghost needs it. You, yourself, may need it. The element of attention lies at the center of the ghost's being. That is the hunger, and this often comes from early on.

There is a fear of abandonment for many like them. Abandonment usually implies being left physically alone, but this is not quite sufficient. The real Hell is to be forgotten.

我們大多數人寧願選擇分心而不是退卻。

...

外部運動導致人們以中心為根。

Wǒmen dà duōshù rén nìngyuàn xuǎnzé fēn xīn ér bùshì tuìquè.

...

Wàibù yùndòng dǎozhì rénmen yǐ zhōngxīn wèi gēn.

67

LETTING THE ROOT SPOIL

We most of us would rather choose distraction than retreat.

So…no rest.

Exterior movements cause one to eschew the center as the root.

We stand in stark defiance of our Destiny, our 命 (Ming), and so, it begins to rot…

"I do it *my* way!"

Each of us sinks into myopia, preferring to move outward than to see the world as we are in it.

EACH OF US IS GIVEN A FINITE AMOUNT OF TIME DURING WHICH TO LIVE BODILY UPON THIS EARTH. To live bodily upon this Earth requires, at some level, that there is a center. An anchor, some place whence nourishment comes and to which our minds can return. This allows us to both contemplate and also act upon the complexities of life.

In ancient Chinese thought, each of us possesses a path, a way of being bestowed to us at birth—a "Mandate of Heaven" (tiān mìng, 天命). With this, each of us is given an imperative which absolutely must be met. The degree to which this individual fate or destiny (ming, 命) occurs depends largely upon the efforts of the individual and the circumstances surrounding the individual.

The more attention paid to meaning, especially one's own, the better prepared for the world, one becomes. This requires that one is able to return back to one's center. To give and receive nourishment, to live, and to grow.

The living ghost does not listen to this internal drive. It does not listen to the Mandate of Heaven, which it had received. Here, the ghost works to achieve bliss, to understand, and to achieve meaning, only as an exteriorized process. This is being driven to distraction.

Flashing signs, notifications, playlists, video clips, and indecipherable noise. All of these can have a role in proper function, proper acquisition of knowledge, and even the realization of one's own path. It is when these things occur as obstacles to this state that the situation becomes problematic.

The living ghost usually faces one of two situations. In the first case, the ghost has spent little time trying to find its way. In the second case, the ghost has turned its back on its own destiny. The first case is somewhat less severe as it often requires only that one have the want to explore, and the resources to do so, although for many this is difficult enough.

The second case is somewhat more troublesome. Here, the ghost has been shown some glimmer of meaning, but is not willing to pursue it.

In either case, given enough time, if one's destiny or allotted mission or talent goes unfulfilled, the heart/mind, or xīn (心) becomes slowly turned backward, and transformation into a living ghost will begin to occur.

There is a secondary state with regard to this passage. This is the state in which the living ghost feels that it is on the proper path, that it is, in fact, realizing its destiny (ming, 命).

This is self-deception.

Here, the ghost clings to its idealized version of destiny in such a way that there is no flexibility of movement within one's own life. There is little, if any room for the cultivation of the self apart from this process. Social and familial interactions may suffer. Activities necessary to sustain the individual become secondary. The heart and the eyes begin to dull. All energy is expended in the realization of some goal. The person becomes driven by their perceived path.

The difference lies in whether the person is nourished by its way of being. If a person is hollowed out by his or her activities, this would not be considered one's true human Destiny. The Human path energizes the individual. This is the difference between a deep love for one's life and infatuation with its trappings. As with so many other aspects of ghostly existence, this sense of destiny many of us possess is but an illusion.

聲音很大，你會發現空耳朵。

你忘記了自己內心的豐滿。

Shēngyīn hěn dà, nǐ huì fāxiàn kōng ěrduǒ.

Nǐ wàngjìle zìjǐ nèixīn de fēngmǎn.

68

TO REVEL IN VIRTUE

Spirituality, profundity, and clarity are yours to display, so much window dressing in an unfinished house...

So willing to speak your truth and running mazes to justify it.

With loud voice you find empty ears.

You forget the fullness of your own heart.

This fullness leaves you with anxiety which you attempt to drown out with the sound of your own surety.

THERE ARE "SPIRITUAL SEEKERS" WHO HAVE TAKEN AS THEIR DESTINY THE SEARCH FOR AND REALIZATION OF UNKNOWN THINGS, OF "INNER PEACE," OR OF MINDFULNESS. These ghosts are so driven to live consciously that they often overpower the consciousness of others. This is driven by righteousness.

This ghost will speak often and in great detail about its own progress along its chosen spiritual path. It may even have an eye toward conversion of others onto its own path. They evangelize in the name of helping such "unfortunates" to reach the point of realization that the ghost itself has attained.

Well-meant but often overbearing, this approach may serve to push others away from the pursuance of self-cultivation as a whole, serving to reinforce that the ghost alone has an understanding of itself and of a reality to which others are just not privy.

This living ghost is one of the most difficult to spot. Violence, defensiveness, and greed are qualities which can be sussed out with relative ease. It is precisely because it wears the garb and bears the marks and uses the language of one who should, by most lines of thought, be immune to its own ghostly nature. Ghostliness, however, is to some extent, an outcome of some of the darker and more repressed aspects of human existence. In many cases, these ghosts seek to "move past" their own human nature, and therefore slip very quickly from the path of an upright, healthy human onto the path of the living ghost.

用細長的手抓住，沒有任何感動⋯

Yòng xìcháng de shǒu zhuā zhù, méiyǒu rènhé gǎndòng...

69

FORGETTING THE MYSTERIOUS

The Way of the Ghost is one of forgetfulness and doubt.

That which cannot be seen or heard is tantamount to a deep-seated lie.

Grasping with slow spindly hands, nothing is touched…

Meaninglessness is anathema in concept.

Yet many of us find this a holy word to be embodied and glorified.

ANY DEEPER MEANING TO LIFE IS HELD TO BE A HARMFUL ILLU-SION, ACCORDING TO THIS GHOST. The proper means by which to conduct oneself in the world is only to acknowledge that which is directly held in the hands or observed by the eyes. To do other than this is to spread lies to others, even if those "lies" provide a deeper meaning for others.

Many ghosts however have nothing short of myopia when it comes to issues of meaning. Those of us who find ourselves in this condition do not seek meaning. It is not even a possibility for many of us. In addition, there is often a tendency to bill any sort of move by others toward that which they considered to be meaningful as useless or as superstitious.

This approach leaves one undernourished, but not in the sense that one might think. If one is to believe that there is no underlying cause or meaning to the world, this is fine. It is a belief. The undernourishment occurs when the ghost begins to miss out on social interaction because its beliefs are so deeply held that they preclude one from interacting with others who do not believe as they do. This may be one who only values the process and praxis of science, but laughably, this too is the work of the religious zealot.

對體現存在的厭惡和羞恥標誌著你的生活方式。

你讓這些黑暗的情緒餵養你，因為你可能會以自己的糞便為食。

Duì tǐxiàn cúnzài de yànwù hé xiūchǐ biāozhìzhe nǐ de shēnghuó fāngshì.

Nǐ ràng zhèxiē hēi'àn de qíngxù wèiyǎng nǐ, yīnwèi nǐ kěnéng huì yǐ zìjǐ de fènbiàn wèi shí.

70

LOATHING AND SHAME

Staring at yourself, you find a body.

Pale,
bloated,
pasty—
in the mirror of your own mind.

Participation in being becomes tiresome, stagnant and boring in this strangest of mortal coils.

Making the body different cannot help, as beauty begets ugliness.

Loathing and shame for the embodied existence mark your approach to life.

You let these darkened emotions feed you as one might feed on one's own feces.

IT IS COMMON FOR ONE TO FIND AN IMPERFECTION IN THE WAY THAT ONE LOOKS OR THE WAY THAT ONE THINKS. There is no being that we can comprehend which exists as perfect in this world. Even still, it is human, even humane to find some joy in one's being—some happiness with oneself even if one is imperfect in one's own eyes.

The eyes of the ghost are clouded over. What it sees is not what others tend to see. As such, many ghosts do not see things as they are, and are keen to recognize those things about themselves which they themselves hate. For many of us, a glance in the mirror can be an exercise in existential angst. We are ill at ease within our own bodies, and even more uneasy within our own minds.

Being that many of us seek to be perfect, it can be little surprise that we are fundamentally incapable of meeting unattainable standards. Again, no one knows what perfect is. The ghost, however, believes it has a pretty good measure of perfection. It often knows that it cannot meet this. Ultimately, the ghost feels as if someone has placed shame upon them and will react in light of the shame. Over time opposing overcomes all other impressions and begins to brush in much more complete strokes and taint the worldview of the ghost. This ghost then begins to work toward freeing itself from what it considers an ugly body and an insufficient mind in whatever way it sees fit. Self-loathing becomes its fuel. Suicide takes on an air of inevitability, and steps toward it may even be undertaken in a misconstrued notion of service to others.

We are not born with this inclination. This stance toward oneself is not altogether human. There is at the root, some deepened wound that occurred when we were at a state of rawness and vulnerability. What may have started as the "smallest" of cuts has become infected and has caused the person to see naught but scars.

274

心臟不安和營養不良，無法發出光彩!

Xīnzàng bù'ān hé yíngyǎng bùliáng, wúfǎ fāchū guāngcǎi!

71

PARTAKING IN DESIRE

A ghost is a creature of the senses.

Beautiful colors and sounds fill the senses with either good or bad and numb all else.

You allow this and encourage it besides.

The heart, disturbed and undernourished, cannot put forth brightness!

AND SO, WE HAVE COME TO DESIRES! This is the stock and trade of the living ghost, and they are a waypost on the Path.

As the loathing (either toward self or others) becomes stronger, the ghost must necessarily numb the feeling or risk inflicting repeated harm upon oneself psychologically. This is when the gnawing hunger begins to grow. Each ghost is different, but each possesses the hunger, and each must attempt to satiate it according to its own desires. The living ghost works to distract itself with fulfillment of the desires so that its own hunger is satiated for some little time.

Often, this takes place in the realm of sensory perception. Overload is the only acceptable approach to fill the void at its core. As time passes, the senses are stretched and pulled far beyond their normal capacities, and since the living ghost is often subject to its own illusions, these illusions become all-powerful and all the more pervasive. It is our desires which give us a compass when we find ourselves lost, as we living ghosts cannot easily hear the call of the heart.

In Chinese thought, the heart only seeks the truth, and if it receives as its only nourishment a repeated glut of illusion and sensory input, it cannot remain healthy for long. Further, because the heart is the home of the Shen spirit, the Shen will be disturbed as well.

It is healthy to retreat from sensory input for some period of time in order to turn inward. The ghost, however, is terrified of silence. It will avoid this quiet self-reflection as one might avoid a plague.

活著的鬼魂被自己的無常而不是自己的幽靈本質
所震驚。

它會採取任何措施來避免這部分生活⋯

Huózhe de guǐhún bèi zìjǐ de wúcháng ér bùshì zìjǐ de yōulíng běnzhí suǒ zhènjīng.

Tā huì cǎiqǔ rènhé cuòshī lái bìmiǎn zhè bùfèn shēnghuó...

72

FEAR OF NON-EXISTENCE

There is a point at which one will see the emptiness of things.

An Abyss which lies just beyond the realm of the five sense, but only just.

In this place is the knowledge of non-existence.

The dreaded Truth that is Death.

The Ghost is terrified by this.

The living ghost is more deeply horrified by its own impermanence than by its own ghostly essence...

It will seek by any measure to avoid this part of life...

Death is the fruit of the Tree of Life.

IN POPULAR CULTURE, THE GHOST EXISTS BECAUSE IT IS INCAPA-
BLE OF ABANDONING FULLY ITS BODY OR ITS HABITUAL SPACES.
It is not ready to go. It is, though, only an energetic husk of its former self. The living ghost is just the same. The living ghost clings to
life. Its fear is not always of death, which is generally interpreted as a
cessation of bodily function. Rather, it is petrified of no longer existing as a conscious being. For many, the loss of consciousness at all is
considered a defeat, or at the very least, something which ought to be
forestalled as long as possible.

Often, heroic measures are employed in order to maintain a firm
hold on waking life. For the living ghost it is frequently the only aspect of life that holds any weight at all.

Unfortunately, the living ghost will not come so easily when
Death arrives. Even with sickened body and faltering mind, the ghost
will still find strength to cling to its fading existence. This state also
insures the living ghost is not far removed from the disembodied
ghost with which we are so familiar. The living ghost spends a great
deal of energy forging the bonds which may later yoke it to the Earth
as an itinerant spirit, for it cannot look into the valley-abyss.

所有事物都具有鮮明的本質。

…

機會和混亂都是全部！

Suǒyǒu shìwù dōu jùyǒu xiānmíng de běnzhí.

...

Jīhuì hé hǔnluàn dōu shì quánbù!

73

There are two approaches to existence for the Ghost, each around meaning revolve...

The first, to search for meaning in every thought, being, and thing.

All things are of a portentous nature.

The second, that all exists without any meaning whatsoever.

Chance and chaos are All!

On either side vitality and energy is squandered and clarity clouded.

The Ghost must begin to act to gain control of either of these prospects.

HERE AGAIN, WE ENCOUNTER THE SEARCH FOR MEANING WHICH VEXES MANY GHOSTS. Broadly speaking there is either no meaning at all to anything whatsoever or there is meaning to be found in every event no matter how miniscule.

Several of the previous passages have discussed the nature of meaninglessness to the ghost, and this is certainly one way that the living ghost approaches issues of meaning, but for some, there is a second way which can be even more insidious. Many of us ghosts would latch onto any situation in order to find any small bit of meaning contained within the intricacies of a given encounter. It is mostly a matter of participation. It is natural for humans to find patterns.

It is natural that one should want to find meaning. This is not ghostlike behavior. The way of the living ghost is to cling to this meaning so that it reinforces what we ghosts already know to be true for ourselves. Herein lies the difference and the point of delineation between the human response and that of the living ghost. Either approach becomes viable in the search for meaning—denial or divination are the same!

鬼的特點是慣性和習慣性。

Guǐ de tèdiǎn shì guànxìng hé xíguàn xìng.

74

The Ghost is characterized by inertia and the habitual.

This inertia can affect the Mind (Shen) as Apathy.

This is a madness caused by immobility, which finds itself rehearsed time and again.

The practice of apathy also spreads to others who find themselves as Ghosts: numb, virulent, and paralyzed.

IN THE PROLONGED SITUATION OF OVERWHELMING ODDS OR IN-SURMOUNTABLE WORK MANY LIVING GHOSTS WILL SIMPLY SHUT DOWN. More than this, the living ghost may begin to fully accept its fate as a living ghost. In this prolonged case, concern brought to bear as a means to motivate change within will fall upon deafened ears. Apathy toward oneself will eventually be directed toward the outside world. This apathy in relation to the self indicates an advanced ghostly state which will eventually impact the external world.

An even greater indicator of one's state is when one begins to have apathy about the well-being of others, especially those close to us. To have concern for others is a humane response and showing it even more so. Apathy, at its root, is lack of concern even in the face of extraordinary circumstances, which can damage relationships, both with others and the self.

A word of caution for all of us. Indifference, consistently practiced, is akin to black magic. It can backfire on you. Spectacularly.

尋找這些腐敗的空間，

無論走到哪裡都要沉重。

鬼知道抑鬱症，暴力，當它去尋找巢穴之間的所有事情。

Xúnzhǎo zhèxiē fǔbài de kōngjiān, wúlùn zǒu dào nǎlǐ dōu yào chénzhòng.

Guǐ zhīdào yìyù zhèng, bàolì, dāng tā qù xúnzhǎo cháoxué zhī jiān de suǒyǒu shìqíng.

75

CORRUPTION IN SURROUNDINGS

You find yourself in strange environs,

Drawn to places either filled with filth or exceedingly clean.

No matter.

Heavy with corruption and stagnation,

Stale water gathered at the bottom of an old jar.

Even if the vessel looks clean, the Ghost knows the contents,

Seeking out these corrupt spaces.

Making heaviness wherever it goes.

The Ghost knows depression, violence, and all things between when it goes looking for a haunt.

This breeds malevolence over time.

If unchecked, it will consume self and system.

"LIKE ATTRACTS LIKE." The activities to which we dedicate ourselves and the environments in which we find ourselves will affect how we exist within the world.

The living ghost is usually a creature of extremes, and the places which we ghosts frequent also tend to exhibit extremes. Dark corners and foreign bodies or bright, industrial sterility both provide a welcoming space for the living ghost.

It is common to have places that one frequents with regularity. Familiarity is a source of comfort, after all. When we can only envision ourselves within our chosen space to the point of excluding other possibilities, it has become a point of focus for our ghostly side, and will sustain it. The prospect of quitting our haunts can produce anxiety deep within us, as we are left vulnerable. Often, like-minded ghosts can be found in these environments, and if we can tolerate company, it will serve to reinforce those habits, thoughts, or situations which contributed to the initial steps along the path of the ghost.

We've all been to a place that made the hairs on the back or neck stand up, or the skin begin to crawl. There are places that one might go to experience fear, shock, or filth. Living ghosts enjoy this, as it means that a certain environment and that certain reactions to this environment are the norm, and are repeated over and over. One may easily imagine going into a dingy building and feeling the heaviness that hangs as one walks down the corridors. One may easily retain the sights, sounds, and smells of a filthy bar, its windows rarely open, and patrons clinging desperately to their drinks. Laboratories open, bright, gleaming, and cold engender dark imagination. Ghosts will find ghosts.

Sequestered spaces beget darkened minds, as new Yang rarely enters, leaving a vacuum within which the Yin will flourish. Too much life, too much warmth, too much Yang drives out the Yin and deprives a ghost of its rest and privacy. Excess is the dual enemy of both health and humanity as well as darkness and staid stillness.

鬼不為別人而活，不能活自己。

Guǐ bù wéi biérén ér huó, bùnéng huó zìjǐ

76

DIMMED RADIANCE

The Ghost cares not about the state of its Light,

Nor the interplay of Heaven and Earth.

The Ghost does not live for others, and cannot live for itself.

The spirit is weakened and cannot come through the eyes.

Radiance slowly diminishes, and eyes sink and darken.

LIVING BEINGS PROJECT A FORM OF LIGHT OR "BRIGHTNESS" (MING, 明) THAT INDICATES A GENERAL STATE OF HEALTH AND VIGOR. Plants project this by the color, size, and shape of their fruits, flowers, and foliage. It is further exhibited by the speed and robustness with which they grow. Animals show it in much the same way. In addition, many animals, including humans will exhibit the state of their míng, by the level of attentiveness and involvement that they show to the external world.

In Chinese thought, humans have a special place in the order of nature. Specifically, in Taoist thought, we are endowed by Heaven with capacities and faculties that no other creature on the earth exhibits. One of these faculties is a much more fully developed spirit in the form of the Shen.

When properly nourished through food and social interaction the Shen will shine through in the eyes, and the person will behave in a way that is appropriate to his or her situation and status, will act with integrity, and will treat others human beings in a meaningful and humane fashion. The Shen will then be able to act in its full capacity, allowing the person to fully and meaningfully interact with the external world and other entities found within it.

The brightness projected by the Shen spirit lets others know that the Shen is fully resident within the body and that they are recognized by that Shen. This light, this radiance only fully occurs when one is properly nourished. If a person is severely malnourished during its younger years, he or she is more likely to have diminished radiance. The bar for homeostasis is set much lower in this case, and if precautions are not taken, may be more likely to become an unwitting traveler on the path of the ghost. The living ghost still suffers from malnourishment in many respects. It may get good food, but the essential social negotiations which must take place are often lacking, and this is just as much malnourishment as is limited access to clean food.

The Shen and thus the radiance of the living ghost are in somewhat different states, and those states are largely dictated by the distance that one has traveled down the path of the ghost. In most cases, the spirit is somewhat obscured. In others, gone altogether. The living ghost does not safeguard its light. Those around it can see, or at least sense that the internal state of the individual is somehow compromised. The living ghost does not always care about its own Radiance. The reason for this lies in the concern for illusion.

Ghosts hold to their own views and perceptions. They do not recognize these views as illusions. Worse, they recognize their own self-imposed views as the only reality. Any Radiance that they do recognize within themselves is very often the product of one of these illusions.

This is the case even if the mind itself is quite sharp. One can have a mind that is predatory, which allows it to react quickly, but whose capacity to interact with other beings may still be lacking, the light of the eyes dulled, or even absent.

Others easily recognize the dull countenance. This is a litmus test. If one is not radiant, this causes others to be ill at ease, to shy away or to even mistrust the ghost.

殣

你，鬼，都讓你的谷靈餓死！

那些應該被封存起來以便保存的東西會被燒掉。

值得歡迎的應該受到歡迎。

Nǐ, guǐ, dōu ràng nǐ de gǔ líng èsǐ!

Nàxiē yīnggāi bèi fēngcún qǐlái yǐbiàn bǎocún de dōngxī huì bèi shāo diào.

Zhídé huānyíng de yīnggāi shòudào huānyíng.

77

THE SICKENED SPIRIT

You, Ghost, have let your Valley Spirit starve!

That which should be sealed up for preservation is frittered away.

That which ought be kept at bay is welcomed.

This is Heaven and Earth in body realized, and it is gravely ill.

IF ONE DOES NOT PROJECT RADIANCE, THIS MEANS THE SHEN IS ILL. This, in turn, often means that the heart itself is compromised. Remember that in Chinese thought, the heart houses the Shen and the Shen projects outward as: consciousness, vibrant thought, and personal carriage.

If these three aspects are not fully realized, other more abstract areas of human thought will begin to suffer. The drive for creativity and beauty will fall by the wayside. The want of novelty and play will begin to dry up. Laughter becomes nonexistent, or even worse, it comes to express only either irony or schadenfreude. The misfortune of others becomes food for the living ghost at this point and humaneness nearly vanishes.

The living ghost may reach a point of inhumanity at which meaning and desire for stimulus become confounded. Often, this is a reaction to hopelessness. At this point, the ghost may not see itself as capable of changing. Or it may have such a strong will to exist that it does not want to change, even in the face of the suffering that it has inflicted.

This is like an animal, wounded to its core, or a demon who delights in the misfortune of others and the chaos ensuing from it. Both are very dangerous. One may harm the body; the other the spirit.

Even this living ghost deserves compassion, though! We are not born into this, and were pushed as from behind during our first clumsy steps on the Path, and often even too young to comprehend the insult we were receiving from those who went before us.

鬼是赞成的鬼。

Guǐ shì zànchéng de guǐ.

78

Nature cares not for the individual, there are no favorites.

Rewards come from meritorious behavior.

Punishment comes from untoward behavior.

For Ghosts, it is the same, except...

The Ghost is the favored of the Ghost.

THE INVETERATE GHOST THAT VENTURES THIS FAR DOWN THE PATH WOULD SURELY HAVE HAD MANY ENCOUNTERS WITH APATHY, CLINGING, LONELINESS, DESIRE, AND HUNGER. The ghost is pulled along the currents of desire and hunger, trapped within numerous eddies of apathy, clinging, and loneliness which suck one down, as it drowns in despair.

It is in this space that the living ghost begins to mete out both punishment and reward to itself. The ghost's reward is the brief satiation of its hunger for a short time, mollified by the tethers and fetters which bind the living ghost to the world. Its punishment is the realization that the Self needs the Hunger. It now recognizes the drive responsible for its consumption. Either of these can cause deeply held damage, which cannot help but leave psychological scars on the mind of the individual. Both reward and punishment can contribute to continued psychological damage, further scarring the ghost.

生命鬼道是飢餓，儘管豐富，無法使用空虛。

Shēngmìngguǐdào shì jī'è, jǐnguǎn fēngfù, wúfǎ shǐyòng kōngxū.

79

HAVING NO VITALITY THROUGH SUBSTANCE

The Way of the Living Ghost is that of starvation despite abundance, an unusable emptiness.

It requires one to hollow out the self in order to keep moving.

Blending into the grey world just to assure its continued survival...

IN TRUTH, WE LIVING GHOSTS FIND THE MEANS TO SUSTAIN THE CORPOREAL BODY EVEN AS WE VERY OFTEN PUSH IT PAST THE LIMITS OF WHAT THE BODY AND SPIRIT ADVISE. This must happen, else the living ghost would transition to the realm of the dead.

The food, water, and air we take in is used in the promotion of growth and the establishment of homeostasis in the body. For the living ghost, it is difficult to effectively utilize the resources that are provided.

This is starvation. The ghost must therefore take from itself in order to keep going. Muscle and fat get sacrificed in order to keep the organism alive in conditions of starvation. In this case emotion, humanity, and novelty are sacrificed in order to maintain the ghostly nature of the individual. After the exhaustion of these meager reserves, a ghost begins to draw resources from others whether they are willing to provide it or not.

It is at this point that the living ghost will begin to syphon away vitality from those around it, and its skin stays rosy and its eyes sparkling while those around it will become ever more pekid, sickly, and fatigued. At this stage, the living ghost has learned that it can take, directly, from the energetic resources of others. Bear in mind that the ghost often does not keep this glow, for the energy it receives most often goes to feed the Hunger in its gut. It is still as hollow as ever.

在一個案例中，活鬼是喧鬧的。

在另一方面，只有一聲無聲的尖叫聲。

Zài yīgè ànlì zhōng, huó guǐ shì xuānnào de.

Zài lìng yī fāngmiàn, zhǐyǒu yī shēng wúshēng de jiān jiào shēng.

80

ON THE QUIETUDE OF THE GHOST

Some ghosts will brag about their needs, their deeds, and their standing.

Their voices ring loud but hollow. They prize their treasures as enduring.

The passions of the heart valued above the content of the heart.

Other ghosts suffer in a different way.

Their voices minuscule or silent.

Here, sunken shoulders and wringing hands as they try not to offend—if they move at all.

Still other ghosts have an even harder way.

Their quietude comes about because there is so much noise that the mind shuts off.

The spirit and soul may leave, or worse, will be trapped within.

In one case the living ghost is trapped in its own muted cries.

In the other, there is only a silent scream.

THOSE OF US WHO HAVE PROGRESSED FAR DOWN THE PATH NO LONGER HAVE THE MEANS TO BRING IN NEW EXPERIENCES. Their mindset will not allow for novelty. At this late stage, there is an abundance only of psychological noise. This noise fills the ghost to the point of psychological and psychic rupture. This we can call "quiet," but it is often so loud that nothing can be heard. This is one of the furthest points on the Path of the Living Ghost, and one which almost always requires a particular or singular event to cause this level of existential descent.

It is a sign of madness, either emergent or entrenched. This living ghost requires great care, as it is teetering precariously on a precipice in its own mind. If left to itself, the ghost will fall backward into the oblivion. And it will lock eyes with you all the way down.

美需要醜陋

善良需要邪惡

困難和輕鬆需要彼此

上下，相同

純潔與污穢合作。

Měi xūyào chǒulòu

shànliáng xūyào xié'è

kùnnán hé qīngsōng xūyào bǐcǐ

shàngxià, xiāngtóng

chúnjié yǔ wūhuì hézuò.

81

ON CULTIVATION

The ghost cultivates itself through many means.

The primary way that it does so is through a "self" consciousness.

This requires that one think in categorical opposites:

Beauty needs ugliness.

Good begs evil.

Difficulty and ease require one another.

Above and below, the same.

Purity partners with filth.

The ghost will find itself on one side or the other,

And in truth, this will usually be assertion or ennui.

THERE IS ONE THING THE LIVING GHOST TRULY CULTIVATES. Division. The ghost views the world as a relationship between self and other, with the qualifier that self and other are not truly related and never will be in any case. To the ghost, boundaries are sharp and absolute, and are never under any circumstances to be dissolved. This gives the living ghost the luxury of both distance and of possession.

The ghost knows the world as a series of opposites which can never fully interact, can never fully transform, and can never fully allow for the growth of both simultaneously. One of the greatest attributes of a living ghost is its hunger, the painful, gnawing sensation in its gut. Since it is able to divide the world into polar opposites, the ghost can separate itself from its hunger. The hunger becomes an external process which it feels it cannot control. In truth, this hunger is the self consuming the Self from the inside as an ouroboros swallows its own tail.

This stage represents the mastering of the rituals used in the attempt to sate the Hunger of the living ghost. These rituals we often learn from other ghosts who are further down the Path than we are. These help to establish us, to birth us into the world as living ghosts. Even here, though, we may be unaware of our plight.

我們這麼多人站立，鬆弛下巴，白內障眼睛，

直到有一瞬間被盜，苦澀，刺耳的呼吸。

Wǒmen zhème duō rén zhànlì, sōngchí xiàbā, báinèizhàng yǎnjīng,

zhídào yǒuyī shùnjiān bèi dào, kǔsè, cì'ěr de hūxī.

82

REALIZATION OF THE WAY OF THE GHOST

The Way of the Ghost is such that one may not know…

It is a Way that cannot be reasoned into, only realized.

In itself, it has no proper name, but a thousand vulgar epithets.

So many of us stand, slack-jawed, and with cataract eyes,

Until there is a moment of stolen, bitter, raspy breath.

We know, at that moment, that we too, now travel on the Way of the Living Ghost—*Shēngmìngguǐdào*.

PARTING REMARKS

According to Chinese folk custom, the number four is considered unlucky. This is because the number four (四) is a homophone for the word for "death" (死) in the Chinese language, both of which are pronounced as "si." Death is the culmination of the human life-cycle as we understand it, and so, it is somewhat fitting that this might be the fourth and last chapter in this book.

Hopefully, it is clear to the reader that this text is not about the metaphoric process of becoming a specter or a serial creature of the night. No. This work is about those of us who have been hollowed and compromised, either through our own choices made within a psychic space of illusion, or as the result of a fundamental, deep, and scarring invasion of the soul. With that in mind, however, this state of affairs is something of a prerequisite for becoming an intangible spirit yoked to the Earth, such as are encountered in nearly all cultures around the world.

Compassion, forgiveness, grace. These are not often mentioned in this text. They are, however, major themes in this text. The reader may find it strange that these "major themes" are not mentioned until what amounts to the conclusion of this book. That is done precisely and purposefully. These final pages are the culmination of the earliest passages of this text. In truth, the reader should know that acknowledgment of the Path of the Living Ghost is not the end, but only the beginning. Throughout the text, it is hoped that the reader had asked him or herself a vital question: "Do I recognize some ghostliness within me which must be rectified?"

If any sense of unwavering clinging is found, if inertia sits upon one's chest, forestalling any newness, or if there is a relentless hunger is to be found within, if there is some fundamental recognition of impairment of care for oneself and connection with self or others, or that one is not truly letting the brightness of spirit shine through, then what will be your next steps?

Will you, ghost, trudge on, body and mind stiffened by your own failure to attend to individual self and to the world? Will you continue to take in the faintest wisps of sustenance—barely clinging to your own humanity? Or perhaps you are only beginning to see the first effects of stagnation or inertia.

This book is the *nigredo*, the *Gu,* the spiritual rotting and recognition of disintegration which must take place in order for the being to transform. It is here where entropy must finally reach its ultimate conclusion. In Daoist ways of thinking, entropy contains the seeds of creation and vice versa, and it is this darkest space herein embodied by the path of the living ghost which will allow one to approach in full honesty the nascent pinpoint of light which can lead the individual back to the path of the human being.

There are three Truths found in Buddhist teachings which illustrate the notion of ghostly behavior to a great extent. These truths are: suffering, craving, and impermanence. These are readily available throughout this text. Indeed, they form the twisted spine of the path.

In the context of the "living ghost," the recognition of impermanence and suffering resides at the center of craving. Craving is the hunger in the pit of the belly, waiting as it is, to be fulfilled. Craving can never reach a state of fulfillment, however. There will always be some new object of focus, or a renewed focus on the same repetitious turn.

It is not enough to recognize these truths which Buddha laid out as abstract concepts. One must use these as an impetus to act in such a way that his or her own humanity is recognized as valuable, particularly in a self-reflective sense.

The subsequent texts to this book will point the reader toward behaviors that exist not as expressions of ghosts or of ghostliness, but of humaneness and humanity. It is only then that one can begin to set aside the nearly innate training which began from an early age which inculcated in many of us the craving and suffering which marks the ghostly experience, and which subsequently set many of us, like a toddler having her first steps, onto the path of the living ghost.

To this end, there will be exercises which may be physical in nature, psychic in nature, or even social in nature which will, it is hoped, help the individual in regaining some sense of humaneness, humanity, and interaction with both self and others. It is in this second text that the reader will find exercises meant to facilitate transformation.

It is a common approach for those of us on the path of the living ghost to try to achieve some victory, some decisive triumph over our "lesser natures," be that the ego, the libido, the shadow, or whatever label one may give it. This is a trap, however. Transformation is the goal. One needs to be careful, as triumph and transformation are two very different things.

If you, the reader, find that it is necessary that you triumph over your ghostly nature, that you conquer it, or that you destroy it—take a good look! You may have settled into yet another ghostly illusion. Transformation is a much longer process, and one which takes both time and proper circumstance. Some of us experience a life-changing event, be it the birth of a child, the death of a beloved parent, or some instance of grievous harm to self. This can be enough to precipitate change for some, even one so entrenched as a living ghost. Most of us, however, require steady and consistent work in order to change.

How are we to know then whether we have stepped away from the path of the living ghost? Remember some of the attributes of the ghost: inability to take in nutrients, inability to relate to others, and a lack of "inner light." These are the pre-existing conditions to ghostly behavior. It is also these same attributes, when reversed, which indicate that a person is realizing his or her own human nature.

Any thriving, living, growing, and evolving being requires some form of sustenance which helps to maintain and even foster the being so that it can transform as is necessary for the natural stage in which it finds itself. This is as true for the smallest microorganisms as it is for the largest and most complex lifeforms. All beings must have access to and must participate in that which sustains us. The human being who is in proper relationship with his or her surroundings and his or her body will be able to take in nourishment, assimilate it, and subsequently, synthesize the energy necessary for balanced and sustainable growth, change, and evolution. This concept of nourishment can extend beyond food, though this is certainly the most readily understood form of nourishment.

On the Tip of the Tongue, in Pit of the Belly

There is an oft-quoted bit of folk wisdom which states: "The way to a man's heart is through his belly." I think this is incomplete. I believe the way to nurture anyone's heart must begin with the belly. This is the base upon which all other activities are built. If food is unavailable, or if there is little connection to food, there will be an inhibition of connection to the body itself. This, in turn, sets the tone for all other aspects of physicality and embodiment.

There is a feeling, a certain kind homesickness which only surfaces for most of us when there is a specific smell in the air—a reminder of a flavor of being in the past which, most of us experience only as a ephemeral impression, harkening back as they tend to do to a time of simplicity and innocence, or at the very least, safety. Very often, this is the retained memory of our first instance of being fed and cared for in some manner that has been retained up to the present.

In many cultures, there is a relationship to body and home which begins with food. We feed and are fed. The form of the body originates from this fundamental activity, and it is the first thing we "learn." Impairment at this level compromises not only general well-being, but also the implicit function of the body itself, which then affects every other aspect of being. For a small section of humanity, this of little concern, as is the case with ascetics of various stripes, who choose to forego the body in the pursuit of higher realms of consciousness.

For the rest of us, the integration of food and foodways is one of the first fundamental steps in reestablishing connection to our own humanity, as it provides the basis for physicality, and thus also embodiment. This is even more true for many who find themselves in the state of exemplification of the Path of the Living Ghost. It is not just the food that sustains us, however, for food can be gotten. It is our relationship to it that gives testament to the meaning that holds for us. Often too, it is not the food itself that is the only factor. It is often the people with whom we partake. Indeed, there are other ways to understand nourishment entirely.

Nourishment can come in the form of any activity which allows the individual some form of growth and/or expression. Social relationships allow humans to become part of a larger whole, and any act which allows an individual access to this social arena will nourish us as social beings to some extent. This realization of the social aspect of life is the second major component of humane-ness which is compromised or missing for many who are on the path of the living ghost. This is the dimension of nourishment which comes when we understand not only the company we keep, but how company keeps us.

Most of us who are on participating in our own individual ghostly paths have a semblance of socialization. There is interaction. The problem arises when the interaction is either severely stunted or self-reflected. The first condition requires that the nourishment provided by social interaction is either unavailable to us or is largely deleterious to us. The individual then functions as a wounded animal, ready as it is to strike out at a second's notice, if necessary. In the second case, a being can be socialized, and indeed may be exceptional in this regard, but here, interaction with others becomes analogous to the way that a modern construction worker may look at his or her tools.

The last major element which exists as an indicator of the ghostly journey is the proverbial darkening of the light—the light available to all of us who possess some level of self-awareness and "spirit." This is the Shen mentioned in Chinese culture. This is an outcome of proper nutrition and positive social participation, both of which are necessary to the proper emanation of one's spirit (Shen) and destiny (Ming). Indeed, the Chinese word for brightness is a homophone for destiny, both of which are pronounced Ming. That is, there is a brightness, a lightness, an ineffable sense of emanation which issues forth when one exists in accordance with his or her "deeper calling" which gives an anchor to one's being and gravitas to one's existence rather than gravity visited upon the person by the world.

The traits and experiences laid out this text indicate the performative aspect of clinging, which informs so many aspects of a life of the individual living ghost. It is a clinging to self and to repeated experience, timeworn and thick. These same traits also describe habits in details of a discarnate ghost, with the main difference being one of degree. This is touched upon in the 31st and 43rd passages in the main body of the text. These passages both evoke the image of one who is chained to the earth, and to its earthly existence even when the spirit might push to move on.

From the perspective of Chinese folk culture, the logical outcome of this state of affairs is that one who is inviting a living ghost can very easily transition into the more spectral form of ghost if the situation is not changed in some respect. The living ghost clings to certain aspects of its life, and this clinging will continue stopping even after the physical death of the individual. This is true even if the initial circumstances which led the individual down its present path were not due to actions taken by the individual. In an analogous fashion, one who dies a violent death can leave enough of a psychic residue that he or she will continue to exist after death even if he or she is not at fault.

Here, the discarnate ghost struggles to be heard, and only exists as a shadow of a shadow of what it was when it was alive. Especially when left alone with no human interaction, the ghost loses its humanness over time. What is left unrecognized and unbidden there then arises the quintessential struggle to hold onto the identity it once held in its incarnated existence.

By the same token, the disembodied ghost set up its repetitious routines, and establishes its haunts as a matter of course, as if it had a choice. The ghost in this case will enact either the most oft repeated aspects of its Monday life, or its most emotionally charged moments. Left without the interaction of others, it will continue in this existence until the spectral residue eventually dissipates like so much thick smoke.

The Daoist teacher Ming Liu attributes the earthbound ghost or human spirit as a sort of "lazy P'o" or animating soul. As a living being transitions to death, the P'o reaches a place wherein the body is no longer alive for it to animate, but it is tied to the human existence in such a way that it cannot or will not disappear into the earth as is its fate, according to the more esoteric readings of Chinese folk cosmology. If the P'o does not return to the earth, it will reside in between the worlds and will thus become a ghost.

For some readers, this may be of little consequence, as they may view existence as the space occurring between one's physical birth (and perhaps, even parturition) and one's inevitable death. Other readers, though, find this prospect to be extremely unnerving. If this is the case, it should be an even greater incentive for one to step away from the Path of the Living Ghost. In truth, the living ghost shows just as much or more of a propensity toward "clinging" in the Buddhist usage of the term.

The most impressive difference, perhaps, is that the living ghost, the Shēngmìngguǐ (生命鬼) still has time to return to, and even more pointedly to rejoin the Path of Humanity. It is still capable of growth, and it is still capable of projecting its brightness into the world. Indeed, this is precisely why the term was chosen. In one sense, it does translate to "living ghost." It expresses the meaning of a life lived as a ghost even while alive. In addition, the first two characters of this phrase present the reader with a more nuanced meaning. The term "shēngmìng" consists of shēng (生) and mìng (命) which are broadly taken to mean growth or growing and life, respectively. This first clause, then implies a being who is still capable of growing one's inner light, recognizing his or her calling, and using these to rejoin the world in some way.

✳ ✳ ✳

The follow-up texts to the present work address in much greater detail some of the practices that can be used by an individual embodying ghostly traits to step away from the Way of the Living Ghost. But the realization of the virtue of rén (仁), or "humanity/humaneness" can only occur once steps are taken to pull one's feet from the mud. This second book will be a call to action for all of us who find ourselves on the path. A movement toward a willful action. A defiant action. Often a painfully slow action. But also, a humane act. It is the deliberate work of returning.

Returning

The six lines above constitute the 24th hexagram (Fu) of the Yijing or "Classic of Changes" is most often translated as "Returning." It shows five Yin lines with one Yang line submerged deep underneath, weighted down and frozen within. In many respects, those of us who find ourselves on the Path of the Living Ghost exist in a space wherein its energy is trapped to a degree such that we are unable to extract ourselves from the mud. We would have no yang to bring to bear on our situation. Living ghosts often exist in a way analogous to the second hexagram of the *Yijing*, which consist of a doubled kūn, (坤) trigram, depicted as ☷. Possessing as it does all six yin ("broken") lines, this hexagram is considered the most yin of the *Yijing* hexagrams, and by extension, the most passive and still of its own accord. As such, there is little potential for meaningful and sustained movement, which is the catalyst for change within one's life. The 24th hexagram possesses a single Yang line at its base which signifies the return of Yang into the world, however inchoate and miniscule its expression may be.

This "Returning" signifies a movement toward previous, more innate states of being. This is nothing less than a return to a more human (and again, more humane) state. This is the Path of the Benevolent Person, the *Shànréndào* (善人道), and the follow-up texts to the present volume seek to facilitate this. These works center on the return of the individual human soul. In many cases, one who exemplifies the living ghost has suffered what might be called "soul loss," as it is understood in many cultures around the world including Chinese cultures. It requires the recognition of loss or at least, "lack," but it also requires the recognition of the inevitability of change. If we are to return to the human sphere, then change must be part of that process.

The reader is asked to examine his or her relationship to change, and his or her ability to engage in it. By its nature, change is difficult for those of us who exist as living ghosts and it is uncomfortable because of this. We will find a reason to change, but many more reasons to stay the same. It will also take time, and most of us are not willing to invest our most finite resource not knowing whether there will be a return on the investment. This is precisely why it ought to be done, however. It will add a richness to one's time which may have been obscured—or missing altogether.

The vast majority of the exercises presented in the subsequent volumes will have a component of energy work which must needs to be done in order for the being to return, at its deepest core, to the human(e) place from which it originated. This can either occur on physical and mental levels, when we put in the time and effort to engage and participate in the larger human experience. Of course, this can also take place even on levels which are much more difficult to quantify. These levels have a certain amount of mystery involved and occur primarily at the level of spiritual involvement, if not spiritual evolution, depending on one's particular orientation toward invisible worlds. To this end, both qigong (literally translated as "energy work") and meditation will figure prominently as part of this process. Yoga, taiji, martial arts, and prayer would all find some use here, although it cannot be understated that a particular theological stance, or *any* theological stance is not necessary to cultivate this aspect of the human(e) experience.

Music and art can also serve this role as well, as long as these add to the quality of life for both the individual and for those around it. These pursuits can allow for creativity, spontaneity, expressiveness, perhaps even playfulness, to surface—aspects of life which are often lacking for those who seldom break from routine. Art in music both allow for the expression of pent up energy, emotions, and affectations.

Physical embodiment is one of the key points of recognition which many living ghosts have great difficulty with. As such, exercises aimed at this level of existence will have as their ultimate goal the reëstablishment of a relationship between self and body. To this end,

JOHN ANDERSON

exercise is a key component, but exercise performed mindfully so that the individual gains a sense of being in and with his or her own body. This does not require intensity. What it requires, however, is an awareness. An awareness of one's body within space. An awareness of one's body as means of expression. An awareness of one's body as a catalyst for change in the external world. Mostly, though, it requires painstaking awareness of the body and psyche as a totality.

At the same time, this type of work asks the individual to reevaluate how he or she interacts with various forms of physical nourishment including but not limited to the food and drink that one partakes in. For some, this may require an involvement with the helping professions such as counseling, which may help to address some of the underlying psychological states which contribute to behaviors often directed at oneself. In short, this requires a redefinition of the relationship between the individual and the nourishment which he or she accepts. It should be said, though, that whether it is physiological or psychic, this experience of nutrition and subsequent integration is only half of the equation. Each of us must learn how and when to rid ourselves of that which is no longer needed. This applies to that which no longer serves a purpose, no longer helps the individual evolve. This is nothing more than the process of "letting go." This is easier said than done in many cases. It is here where the person must show both compassion and grace, directed intimately and specifically toward oneself.

Still other exercises will call upon the individual to involve him or herself in some form of social exercise so that he or she can establish proper relationships with other vibrant and growing humans (as well as other beings who can further add to the evolving narrative of the individual). Social involvement is another of the keys to this process of humanity or Ren (仁), which lies at the center of the social human experience, as well as society itself. Key to this process will be acts of service, such as volunteering in its various forms, especially when it involves direct and fulfilling human contact.

Each of these is part of what it means to be human—whether this is an involvement with self as a body, involvement with others as a social being, or an involvement with the grander schemes of unseen motions such as when one recognizes the brightness that he or she lets shine through to the world, and the root of these lies in awareness, both of oneself and of others.

In some senses, this approach is paradoxical considering the stance toward social and societal interaction, which a more philosophical reading of Daoism seems to take. That is, it is often interpreted as the way of the hermit. It is considered the philosophy of an individual extended out into the world. To me, Daoism speaks to universal processes which are embodied, individual experiences, but which also extend far beyond the borders of physicality and "self." It is left to the individual to do a certain amount of internal work, bordering as it often does on the mystical. But the individual is not removed from society in many cases, and indeed religious forms of Daoism work to form congregations. Even in the most extreme cases of seclusion, there seem to be some basic level of human interaction which give rise to the legend of the hermit as a being, formless, yet participating with the world at some unfathomable level which most of us could only hope to attain. The reason why we listen, rapt, to stories of Daoist hermits is so that we, the relatively unenlightened masses can have a point of reference in our everyday worlds. Experience of the Dao can happen in any context if awareness is given and acted upon with sufficient time for change. That is, for some of us the enlightenment we seek comes only after sequestering ourselves from the rest of the world, but for many of us, indeed I think most of us, it comes from opening ourselves up to the world in a particular way, which forces us to be present.

These are certainly only the first steps toward humanity as a state of being. The first steps, returning toward humanity. The first steps returning toward the change, which is an inevitable part of existence. The first steps returning toward our own humaneness extended, both toward ourselves, as the tenderest of self-mercies, and also extended outward toward a world of others who may also find themselves, much too often, in the vice grip of their own ghostly journeys. Herein, too, there can be compassion for the condition of all Living Ghosts, for all of us who are stuck in our experiences to the point of exclusion, or even mired in our own histories to the point of forsaking possible futures, for all who may still yet be able to brighten the world around them. Conversely, there is implied in this text a warning about the grey pall, which can color humanity as we become more distant from each other and ourselves, descending over new generations as well as the slow dampening of the tiny stalwart wick which feeds the light most of us inherently seek. This book is, after all, an exhortation: "Step away, and stumble off the Way of the Living Ghost as best you are able! Grow that which helps you to grow!"

This should not be the end of one's work toward a more evocative and involved existence. Rather, it should be the beginning of the process of cultivating one's own brightness and adding it to the broader human experience that is living in accordance with others, and with oneself.

BIBLIOGRAPHY

The *Daodejing* is considered one of the seminal texts of Daoist philosophy and religion. Attributed to Laozi (also transliterated as Lao Tzu or Lao Tse) and purportedly written in the 6th century BC. In contemporary academic circles, it is widely agreed that the text was compiled over time and by several individuals or groups. Add to this a work whose subject matter is often very abstract, and one can quickly understand why translations of the *Daodejing* being similarly diverse, with each translation presenting a difference in intent, linguistic and semantic focus, and audience.

TRANSLATIONS OF THE *DAODEJING*

Daodejing: The Dao and its Energy. Translated by Richard Bertschinger. https://mytaoworld.com/books/the-dao-de-jing/. 2009.

Lao-Tzu: Te-Tao Ching: A New Translation Based on the Recently Discovered Ma-wang tui Texts. Translated by Robert Henricks. Ballantine Books, 1992.

Tao Te Ching: A New English Translation. Translated by Stephen Mitchell. New York: Harper Perennial Modern Classics, 2006.

Tao Te Ching: The Definitive Translation. Translated by Jonathan Star. New York: Tarcher, 2003.

The Canon of Reason and Virtue: (Lao-tze's Tao Teh King) Chinese and English. Daisetsu Teitoro Suzuki, and Paul Carus. La Salle: Open Court, 1913. http://www.sacred-texts.com/tao/crv/index.htm.

OTHER WORKS

Deng, Ming-Dao. *The Living I Ching.* New York: HarperOne, 2013.

Huang, Alfred. *The Complete I Ching—10th Anniversary Edition: The Definitive Translation.* Rochester: Inner Traditions, 2010.

JOHN ANDERSON

324

Karcher, Stephen and Rudolf Ritsema. *I Ching: The Classic Chinese Oracle of Change [The First Complete Translation with Concordance].* New York: Barnes and Noble, 1995.

Kroll. Paul W. *A Student's Dictionary of Classical and Medieval Chinese Revised Edition.* Leiden: Brill, 2017.

Liu, Ming. "Healing Apprenticeship—Class 7 Possession: TCM and Possession Part One: Basic View." www.dayuancircle.org.

———. "Healing Apprenticeship—Class 8 Possession: TCM and Possession Part Two: Common Prevention." dayuancircle.org.

———. "Healing Apprenticeship—Class 9 Possession: TCM and Possession Part Three: Forms of Treatment." dayuancircle.org.

———. "Healing Apprenticeship—Class 10 Possession: TCM and Possession Part Four: Earth Spirits." dayuancircle.org.

———. "Healing Apprenticeship—Class 11 Possession: TCM and Possession Part Five: Water Spirits." dayuancircle.org.

Liu, Yousheng. *Let the Radiant Yang Shine Forth: Lectures on Virtue.* Translated by Sabine Wilms and Zhuozhi Liu. Freeland: Happy Goat Productions, 2017.

Manser, Martin H., et. al. (Eds.). *Pocket Oxford Chinese Dictionary 4th Edition.* New York: Oxford University Press, 2009.

Noritaka, Kikuchi. "The Accumulation of Crime and Punishment: The Ancient Daoist Notion of "Inherited Burden" and its Relevancy Today." *Journal of International Philosophy.* no.1 (2012): 194–98. https://www.toyo.ac.jp/uploaded/attachment/4800.pdf.

Ritsema, Rudolf and Shantena.Augusto Sabbadini. *The Original I Ching Oracle: The Pure and Complete Texts with Concordance.* London: Watkins, 2007.

Yuan, Boping, and Sally Kathryn Church. *Oxford Beginner's Chinese Dictionary Bilingual Edition.* New York; Oxford University Press, 2005.

Yuen, Jeffrey. Edited and Compiled by Stephen Howard. "3 Souls and 7 Spirits." Newton: New England School of Acupuncture Continuing Education Department, 2005.

About the Author

John Anderson received his Master of Sciences degree from the Florida College of Integrative Medicine in 2009 and his Doctorate in Acupuncture and Oriental Medicine in 2012 from the Oregon College of Oriental Medicine. He has taught all aspects of Traditional Chinese Medicine in schools across the country. He has written on many topics including: Eastern philosophy, Chinese medicine, herbal medicine, and disability studies.

He has been studying and working with the Yijing for nearly twenty years, both as a divinatory system and as a shorthand for understanding the Earth and the broader cosmos around and within each of us.

In his spare time, he can be found smoking cigars, talking with ghosts of various sorts, and peering into the future, though he rarely tells anyone what he sees.

He currently resides in Florida.

About the Series

The Folk Necromancy in Transmission series examines the folk magical expressions and interrelations of the histories, philosophies, and practices of spirit conjuration, ghost-lore, eschatology, charm-craft, demonology, and the mass of rituals, protocols, and beliefs signalled by the terms "nigromancy," "necromancy," and their various equivalents in traditions across the world.

Here we take the canonical and reveal the folkloric expression; here the historical text inspires new practice and discourse. This series will not simply chart the print history of grimoires, or their socio-political context, but explore their actual magical usage. Within this exploration comes discourse on and with those traditions, extant or extinct, deemed 'necromantic' that are passed through oral transmission.

Raising the dead, we acknowledge the raising of necromancy itself, for it is still the breath of the reader that gives new life to the Dead from the bones of old Books. This is a folk necromancy that is at once extant and revived, inspired and yet-to-be. Here we walk hand-in-hand with the patrons of this particular Art.

THE WAY OF THE LIVING GHOST
WAS TYPESET BY JOSEPH UCCELLO.
THE TYPEFACES:
JJANNON, JJANNON DISPLAY,
ADOBE FANGSONG STD,
SKOLAR PE, PINGFANG HK,
KAZURAKI SP2N, AND
GT AMERICA.

CPSIA information can be obtained
at www.ICGtesting.com
Printed in the USA
LVHW060754160919
631186LV00006B/288/P